30 Wilderness Activities to Enjoy Nature Together!

The Family Guide to OUTDOOR ADVENTURES

CREEK STEWART, Author of Survival Hacks

ADAMS MEDIA
NEW YORK   LONDON   TORONTO   SYDNEY   NEW DELHI

Adams Media
An Imprint of Simon & Schuster, Inc.
100 Technology Center Drive
Stoughton, Massachusetts 02072

First Adams Media trade paperback edition May 2023

ADAMS MEDIA and colophon are trademarks of Simon & Schuster.

For information about special discounts for bulk purchases, please contact Simon & Schuster Special Sales at 1-866-506-1949 or business@simonandschuster.com.

The Simon & Schuster Speakers Bureau can bring authors to your live event. For more information or to book an event contact the Simon & Schuster Speakers Bureau at 1-866-248-3049 or visit our website at www.simonspeakers.com.

Interior design by Sylvia McArdle
Illustrations by Tess Armstrong
Photographs by Creek Stewart

Manufactured in China

10 9 8 7 6 5 4 3 2 1

Library of Congress Cataloging-in-Publication Data has been applied for.

ISBN 978-1-5072-2040-5
ISBN 978-1-5072-2041-2 (ebook)

TO MY BEAUTIFUL FAMILY, SARAH, RIVER, AND LAKELYN.
HERE'S TO A LIFETIME OF ADVENTURES!

CONTENTS

Introduction . . . 6

CHAPTER 1

HOW TO ENJOY
NATURE TOGETHER . . . 8

CHAPTER 2

NATURE ART . . . 13

Project 1: Walnut Dye a T-Shirt . . . 14

Project 2: Cast Animal Tracks . . . 18

Project 3: Harvest Your Own Clay . . . 22

Project 4: Make an Aztec
Clay Whistle . . . 26

Project 5: Paint Gnome Rocks . . . 30

Project 6: Weave a Wildflower
Crown . . . 34

CHAPTER 3

FUN AND GAMES . . . 38

Project 7: Leaf Rubbing Journal . . . 39

Project 8: Make a Bull-Roarer . . . 43

Project 9: Weave a Cattail Duck
Decoy . . . 47

Project 10: Make a Tennis Ball
Shepherd's Sling . . . 51

Project 11: Attract Birds with a Pine
Cone Bird Feeder . . . 55

Project 12: Carve an Old Man Face
in a Bar of Soap . . . 59

CHAPTER 4

FORAGING AND FOOD . . . 63

Project 13: Brew Dandelion Tea . . . 64

Project 14: Plant a Milk Carton
Garden . . . 68

Project 15: Make a Vagabond
Stove . . . 72

Project 16: Cook Bacon and Eggs in a
Paper Bag . . . 76

Project 17: Bake Orange Peel Ash
Muffins . . . 80

Project 18: Bake Stick Bread . . . 84

Project 19: Catch Minnows (and
Other Fishing Bait) with
Spiderwebs . . . 88

CHAPTER 5

GEAR AND TOOLS . . . 92

Project 20: Make Pine Pitch Glue . . . 93

Project 21: Make a Plastic Water Bottle
Fish Trap . . . 97

Project 22: Make a Tulip Poplar Leaf
Berry Basket . . . 101

Project 23: Carve a Paint Stick
Hand Reel . . . 105

Project 24: Abrade a Slate
Arrowhead . . . 109

Project 25: Start a Campfire Using
a Ferro Rod . . . 113

CHAPTER 6

WILDERNESS SHELTERS . . . 117

Project 26: Build a Debris Hut . . . 118

Project 27: Make a Quinzee
Snow Shelter . . . 122

Project 28: Erect a Tarp Shelter . . . 126

Project 29: Make Mud and
Straw Bricks . . . 130

Project 30: Lash a Tower . . . 134

Template . . . 139
Index . . . 141

INTRODUCTION

Less screen, more green! In the world of smartphones, tablets, and online learning, the need for children to engage with nature has never been more evident. Outdoor activities and projects inspire exploration, creativity, curiosity, learning, and a sense of wonder. Not only that; interacting with nature also fosters a healthy respect and love for the outdoors. Bottom line: Spending time on projects to help your children get outside and have fun is an investment that will not only strengthen your bond together but will create memories that will last a lifetime!

As an outdoor and survival instructor for over twenty years, I make intentional effort to try to get my kids outside as much as possible. But competing with the fast-paced world of today, where everything is available at the push of a button and usually conveniently wrapped in plastic, isn't easy. You have to get creative and be engaged with your kids. Let them discover the many wonders of nature, the joys of being outside, the silly fun of getting a little dirty—as you have fun and learn together. That time spent together outside cooking by a campfire or casting animal tracks will create moments that will absolutely strengthen any parent-child relationship.

The Family Guide to Outdoor Adventures outlines thirty outdoor projects you can do with your kids. Each project is designed to get you and your kids outside, teach about nature, and be more fun and exciting than any phone or computer screen ever could be! Each project includes an age

level so you can pick the ones best suited to your child, and a Parent's Guide with safety advice and/or tips that will help you reinforce the learning and promote engagement. Inside you'll find projects like:

- Harvesting Your Own Clay
- Weaving a Cattail Duck Decoy
- Attracting Birds with a Pine Cone Bird Feeder
- Cooking Bacon and Eggs in a Paper Bag
- Making a Plastic Water Bottle Fish Trap
- Starting a Campfire Using a Ferro Rod
- Making Mud and Straw Bricks

And as an added bonus, you'll also be teaching your kids a sense of responsibility toward nature and themselves—skills that will benefit them long after the clay has hardened or the paint has dried.

So grab your kid, dig in, get your hands dirty, learn some cool nature facts, complete some awesome projects, strengthen your bonds, laugh, love, make memories, and get out into the wonders of nature! You'll have the time of your lives!

CHAPTER 1

HOW TO ENJOY NATURE TOGETHER

I've never met a kid who doesn't like to play outside. It's true, not a single one. However, the quality of their outside experiences will influence their feelings for the outdoors, positively or negatively. This chapter will help ensure that your experiences outside are positive ones. I've learned through trial and error that a positive experience takes effort and planning. From snacks and cleanup supplies to first aid and attitude, this chapter will present some things to consider before heading outside. These can make a huge difference in the quality of your outdoor experience!

NATURE IS ALL AROUND

There is a misconception that you must be secluded in a remote wilderness off the grid to learn outdoor skills. This couldn't be further from the truth! Most adventures can be had just a few steps from your back door. Don't let a lack of access to vast areas of wilderness stop you from taking your kids outside to have fun. They can often find the excitement of an undiscovered wilderness at the edge of almost any parking lot if they use their imagination. And if you have a yard larger than 6 feet by 6 feet, then you have enough room to go camping and pursue countless outdoor projects. My motto is that the backyard is the perfect place for practicing skills that you might need in the wilderness one day.

No Backyard? No Problem!

When my son was born, we lived in an apartment in the middle of town, with no yard at all. For several years until we moved, a small patch of landscaping between the parking lot and the dumpster was all the jungle we needed. We spent countless hours hidden amongst the rose bushes and decorative grasses learning skills together in our private oasis. My point is that no matter where you live, there are places to spend time outside. You may have to get a little creative, but they are there. For those of you who are urban dwellers, a few ideas include nearby community parks, patches of grass between sidewalks, landscaped areas around apartments, natural areas beside canals and waterways, and the lawns of places where people congregate such as churches.

BE FULLY ENGAGED

This book is not designed to hand off to a kid with a pat on the back and an enthusiastic "Go have fun outside!" *You* are a critical part to this equation. In fact, you're the most important part. Your attitude, enthusiasm, planning, and engagement are at the very center of your child's outside experience, at least in the beginning. Ultimately, you will be the biggest influence in how your child enjoys and appreciates the outdoors. Ask yourself—would *you* want to play with *you* outside?

It's time to channel your inner child for a few minutes and do your best to let go of thoughts about budgets, house chores, work responsibilities, and tomorrow's to-do list. Live in the moment and be present with your child. I've learned that children have a sixth sense and can tell if you're faking interest. So take a deep breath, decompress, and get in the right headspace to have fun!

PREPARE TO GET DIRTY

Your engagement in each project is critical, but it's very likely you might need to lighten up a bit. My wife, who is incredibly clean and tidy, is a perfect example of this. While there isn't anything wrong with adhering to cleanliness around the house, it can be a bit of a downer in terms of outside play. She must make a conscious effort to lighten up and allow our kids to get dirty, splash in the creek, pick up frogs, get sweaty and sticky, and the list goes on. I believe the most fun outside will probably require a shower afterward—maybe even two. In a world dominated by cleanliness and disinfection, permission to "get dirty" outside adds to the adventure of it all in the mind of a child.

KEEP AN EYE ON THE WEATHER

Extreme weather conditions can taint anyone's enthusiasm for outside play. If a child's only experience outside is too hot, too cold, too windy, too icy, too humid, too rainy, or any other extreme, that memory will be ingrained in their brain for a long time. There are always exceptions—running through the sprinklers on a blistering hot day, sledding when it's cold and snowy, and taking rain showers during a downpour—but when it comes to outside projects like those described in this book, it's best to avoid or plan around weather extremes.

There are many ways to work around extreme weather. A nice campfire can solve so many cold weather problems. Heading outside in the mornings and evenings can help avoid the heat of the day. Setting up a canopy or working under a pavilion can give you the best of both worlds when it's raining. But don't force an outside project in extreme weather. It rarely works out and typically leads to frustration, short tempers, and even potential dangers.

There is a saying—"Hope for the best but prepare for the worst"—that is so true when venturing outside. If there is one thing that is predictable about nature, it is that it is unpredictable. Rarely does everything go according to plan. Especially when it comes to the weather, my suggestion is to be ready for anything. This is why planning ahead and having a good assortment of clothing and gear on hand is so important.

YOUR ADVENTURE BACKPACK

Whether you're headed to the backyard, a local park, or the edge of the wilderness, a backpack with a few essentials can go a long way to making sure you get the most out of playing outside. Having a few key items can prevent the need to unexpectedly go back home. Following is a list of several items to consider taking on your adventure:

- **Water:** From drinking to cleanup, water is essential for any outside project. Not having water can drive you back home quicker than just about anything else.
- **Snacks:** Snack breaks can be a necessity in case of unexpected hunger or a delay in returning home, but they can also be a strategy too. You can use snack breaks to break up a project. Snacks help to keep

kids engaged and these short breaks also help to hold their attention longer. Besides, what kid doesn't love a quick snack break?

- **Change of clothes:** It's better to have extra clothes and not need them than need them and not have them! Getting dirty is fun, but trashing the car interior isn't. Having a change of clothes just in case is always a good idea.
- **Extra sweatshirt or jacket:** Whether to cut the chill or cover up from mosquitoes, having one of these on hand is always a good idea.
- **Poncho:** Rain showers can come out of nowhere. Having a lightweight poncho or rain jacket on hand for everyone is really important, especially in colder seasons.
- **Cleanup supplies:** Some wet wipes, paper towels, a bath towel, hand sanitizer, and any other items you can think of for cleanup can be very helpful. You should also consider packing an empty garbage bag (or two) to bring back any trash you create or for wet and dirty clothes.
- **Sunscreen:** A good sunscreen can help prevent regrets tomorrow.
- **Insect repellent:** Bugs, especially mosquitoes and ticks, can instantly ruin an outdoor plan. For most adventures, I use a clothing treatment called Permethrin Fabric Treatment by Sawyer. Permethrin is an insect repellent that is applied to clothing and other fabric gear. It bonds to the fabric fibers for up to six weeks or through six washings (whichever comes first) and is the most effective insect repellent I've ever used. I also carry a mail-in test kit for ticks by www.cutterticktest.com. If anyone in your group happens to get a tick on them, you can mail it with this kit to see if the tick is carrying any diseases. This allows you to get ahead of anything before it becomes an issue. Bugs are a part of playing outside. You can't have one without the other, but you can take some great measures to protect yourself and your kids.

- **Blanket/chairs:** A blanket is great to lay on the ground or across a log. Small camp chairs are also indispensable if you're headed to an area that doesn't have a picnic table or similar amenities. They are inexpensive, lightweight, and portable.
- **First aid kit:** A good first aid kit should include all the basics just in case. A small backpack kit could include a variety of bandages, a variety of gauze, medical tape, blister treatment kit made from gauze and Leukotape, alcohol wipes, wet wipes, a couple of elastic ACE brand of wrap bandages, an EpiPen (in case of an unexpected allergic reaction), tweezers, cotton swabs, portable eyewash system, Combat Application Tourniquet, a tick kit (mentioned earlier), and a few triangular bandages.
- **Headlamp flashlight:** I always pack an LED headlamp flashlight just in case. You can use it to look inside hollow trees and to hike back home at dusk.

STAYING SAFE

While you'll not likely be adventuring too far from the beaten path, I wouldn't be a good outdoor skills instructor if I didn't offer some time-tested safety tips.

- **Share your plans:** The number one rule of outside play is to tell someone where you're headed and when to expect you back. While you never expect to get lost, especially in familiar places, it's possible. That's why you should always share your plans with someone outside your group.
- **Carry a fully charged cell phone:** As Benjamin Franklin so famously penned, "an ounce of prevention is worth a pound of cure." One of the best modern takes on this timeless quote is a fully charged cell phone. The ability to call out can quickly help to mitigate a nasty situation if one arises. And if you have a smartphone, you can also Google answers to questions as they arise about plants, animals, rocks,

and more. Instead of allowing the phone to be a distraction, utilize it as a tool for learning when the opportunity arises. And of course, you can capture photos and videos of your outdoor projects to share with friends and family. Don't forget to include the hashtag #CREEKSTEWART when posting online so I can see them too!

- **Adult supervision:** There are several activities detailed in this book that require adult supervision, especially for younger children. Among them include using a pocketknife and lighting a campfire. While I've listed suggested age ranges for each activity, keep in mind that several will require close adult supervision, and thus more teaching opportunities!

YOUR FIRST OUTDOOR PROJECT

For years I taught outdoor summer library youth programs to thousands of kids. To kick off each session, I always started with teaching how to build a mini survival kit and it was always a highlight of the course. Doing so is also a great way to get in the mindset of heading outdoors. It allows to you to talk about safety, precaution, planning, and the importance of being prepared. Besides, every kid loves packing a small candy tin with tiny "survival items" for the outdoor adventures that lie ahead. Following is a suggested packing list for a child-friendly survival kit that just may come in handy as you embark on the projects in this book. The perfect container for a pocket survival kit like this is an Altoids mint tin.

A pocket survival kit like this one is a great first project to prepare for heading outside.

PACKING LIST

- 1-2 needles protected between 2 small strips of duct tape (optional for younger children)
- Few feet of duct tape wrapped around a short No. 2 pencil
- The inner spool of dental floss
- Variety of bandages
- Magnifying lens for starting a campfire using the sun (available at your local pharmacy)
- Whistle
- Ferro rod for starting a campfire (discussed later) (optional for younger children)
- Small pocketknife (optional for younger children)
- Resealable plastic bag bound together with a rubber band
- Small snack or piece of candy
- Candle

With your adventure backpack ready and your pocket survival kit stashed away, it's time to get started!

Now that you're fully equipped to have a positive experience outside, it's time to have some fun. The outdoor projects on the following pages are divided into five chapters: Nature Art, Fun and Games, Foraging and Food, Gear and Tools, and Wilderness Shelters. In these chapters you'll find projects for kids of all ages and personality types.

CHAPTER 2

NATURE ART

There is no better studio for bringing out a child's inner artist like the outdoors. From painting rocks and harvesting clay to natural dyes and preserving animal tracks, outdoor art projects encourage creativity, individuality, and imagination. Every child is an artist, and Mother Nature provides so many unique mediums, tools, palettes, and materials to work with.

Outdoor art projects engage all of a child's senses and boost self-confidence unlike anything else. A place on the refrigerator is the equivalent to receiving an Olympic gold medal in the mind of a child. Featuring and celebrating their artistic creations provides them with a powerful sense of accomplishment that builds their self-esteem.

A great benefit of utilizing nature in art projects is the opportunity for a child to learn about and become comfortable with the natural world. Nature art is like science class and art class combined into one big fun, creative activity. In addition, heading outside adds a sense of adventure and exploration to what is typically an "inside" activity. The nature art projects in this chapter will require you and your child to go outside in search of inspiration and tools. While a finished work of art is the goal of each project, you'll find the journey getting there to be just as important.

Walnut Dye a T-Shirt

Age: 6+

MATERIALS NEEDED

- Gloves
- 10–20 black walnuts in husks, green or brown
- Large rock
- Large pot
- 1 gallon water
- Campfire, grill, or outdoor stove
- Sieve, colander, or slotted metal spoon
- White 100 percent cotton T-shirt
- Rock (optional)
- Long, sturdy stick

The thick green husk of the black walnut tree can be used at any stage in growth to create an impressive tan to dark brown dye for darkening anything from clothing and wood to skin and leather. This dye works best with 100 percent natural fibers such as cotton and linen. The husks are the exterior green fleshy parts that grow around the hard brown seed (walnut) of the black walnut tree.

The black walnut (*Juglans nigra*) is a large tree, growing up to 120 feet tall. It has deeply furrowed gray bark and large 1- to 2-foot-long leaves with an odd number of leaflets that have serrated edges. The large nuts they produce are a telltale identifying feature. These golf ball- to tennis ball–sized nuts can be found littering the ground around the trees from summer through fall. As fall approaches, all the nuts will drop from the tree and the husks will begin to decompose and turn brown. Black walnut trees can be found in all of the eastern United States and as far west as Utah. For western states, look for a very similar tree called English walnut (*Juglans regia*).

To make a strong colored dye for clothing, it's important to boil the walnut husks in water. Walnut dye makes a wonderful clothing dye that results in the most earth tone shade of brown you've ever seen. This can easily be done in the backyard to turn boring white cotton shirts into uniquely colored, one-of-a-kind garments.

INSTRUCTIONS

Step 1: Put on gloves, then remove the husks from the walnuts by smashing them with a rock. It doesn't matter if the walnuts are fresh off the tree (green) or dried and decomposing on the ground (brown). Both work equally well. The nuts inside can be stored for harvesting the edible nutmeats later.

Step 2: Add the husks to a large pot and cover the husks with water. Place the pot in the coals of a campfire or suspend it over the flames using a tripod. This can also be done on a grill or outdoor stove.

Step 3: Bring the water to a boil and stir to help release the tannins from the husks. Simmer at least 30 minutes. The longer you simmer, the stronger the dye will be.

Step 4: Use a slotted metal spoon or simply a forked stick to carefully remove or strain as many of the husks out as you can.

Step 5: Submerge your T-shirt in the liquid and continue to simmer for about 1 hour. You can use a long stick or a rock to keep the T-shirt fully submerged. Simmering helps to drive the color into the fibers and produces a much longer-lasting dye than cold submersion. Once finished, take out the T-shirt using a stick and spread out on the ground to dry (be careful of hot water). After it is dry, shake off any walnut husk pieces and wash and dry in your home washer and dryer by itself before wearing.

PARENT'S GUIDE

Safety Notes

- The juice within the green husks of walnuts and the resulting liquid when mixed with water will dye virtually *anything*. This includes furniture, decks, pans, skin, clothing, concrete, carpet, and more. I highly suggest doing this project outside in the yard and away from anything you don't want stained or ruined! Wear gloves if you don't want brown fingers for a few weeks.

- Always be extra cautious when working around a campfire and very hot water. Adults should do the stirring while the kids watch.

Tips to Improve Engagement

- Turn this into a walnut tie-dye party. Tie-dying is simply a process where you prevent the dye from reaching certain parts of the T-shirt. This is typically done by crumpling or twisting the shirt and holding it in place using string or rubber bands. The folds and twists will prevent the dye from penetrating the fabric in those areas and create unique patterns.

- The resulting liquid created by simmering walnut husks can be used as a primitive type of ink or paint. Consider using the cooled liquid as a medium for creating a natural painting on canvas or paper.

- Further learning: Would you like to learn more outdoor uses for black walnuts? I've included additional projects on a full-color downloadable PDF at the online resource page for this book at CreekStewart .com/FamilyGuide.

Project 2

Badger
Beaver
Bison
Black Bear
Boar
Coyote
Grizzly Bear
Raccoon
Skunk

Cast Animal Tracks

Age: 3+

MATERIALS NEEDED

- Scissors
- Plastic cup
- Plaster of Paris
- 8 ounces water (per track cast)
- Stick
- Paper clip (optional)
- Permanent marker

Track casting is the process of creating a hard mold of animal tracks in the wild using plaster of Paris. The result is a cool plaster cast of the track that preserves it forever. Over time, you can build a collection of track casts from different animals local to your area. It's a great way to learn animal track identification and even animal behavior. Track casts make great displays on a shelf or even on the wall.

Searching for animal tracks teaches children situational awareness. To find them they must study the ground and be aware of their surroundings. This is a great skill for any child and has applications in nearly every aspect of life. Being observant is oftentimes a learned trait, and searching for tracks is great practice.

Searching for animal tracks in the wild is like an Easter egg hunt. The best places to find good tracks for casting are along the muddy edges of creeks, streams, and ponds. Almost every animal frequents these places for water, so it's not uncommon to find a wide variety of local species. Who knows, you may spot a track that will surprise you, like a mountain lion, a bear, or even Bigfoot!

INSTRUCTIONS

Step 1: The first step is to find your animal track! This is a great opportunity to go on a backyard hike or to the local park. Walk the banks of ditches, creeks, streams, or ponds and look for muddy spots. You'll find one eventually! Once you find a track, gently clear any rocks, sticks, grass, or other debris from around it as best as you can. Use the scissors to cut the top 2 inches off your plastic cup and place this piece as a mold around your track.

Step 2: Use the rest of the cup to mix up your plaster; 2 cups of dry plaster mix should be plenty for most tracks. (A 44-pound box of plaster of Paris can be purchased in the drywall patch section of your local hardware store.) Then add enough water to create a mix that is the consistency of pancake batter. It needs to be a little runny so that you can pour it into the track and mold. Just slowly pour in a little water and stir with a stick. Add water until the mixture is runny enough to pour. Be sure to mix in all of the dry plaster.

Step 3: Cast your track! With the cup rim mold in place, pour your plaster mix all the way around the track. This mix will harden solid in about 30 minutes, so take a half hour to enjoy the surroundings or hunt for more tracks!

Step 4: Cool tip: Before the plaster has hardened, consider inserting a paper clip halfway deep into the plaster. Once plaster hardens, this will act as a hanging loop for your track if you want to display it on the wall!

Step 5: When the plaster has hardened, remove it from the mold to reveal a 3-D cast of the track! The dirt or sand can be brushed away with a little water and an old toothbrush. Record the date and animal species on the back of the track cast with a permanent marker and let this be the start to your new collection.

PARENT'S GUIDE

Tips to Improve Engagement

- What track is this? That will be the first question your children ask when they find an animal track. To help, I've created a free downloadable animal track identification sheet that you can print off and take with you on your search. This sheet includes all the most common animal tracks in North America. You can find it at CreekStewart.com/FamilyGuide.

- Studying animal tracks can be a very fun and engaging hobby. There is so much more to learn than simply what type of animal made the track. When you find tracks, challenge your kids to "complete the story" of the tracks. What was the animal doing? Are there any signs of eating or even a confrontation with another animal? Is there any scat (poop)? If so, can you tell what the animal was eating? What direction was the animal headed? Where do you think it was going? Tracks are not just prints in the mud or sand. They are a record of animal activity, and it is *so much fun* to try to figure out that story.

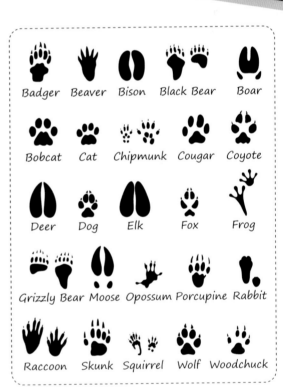

Badger   Beaver   Bison   Black Bear   Boar

Bobcat   Cat   Chipmunk   Cougar   Coyote

Deer   Dog   Elk   Fox   Frog

Grizzly Bear   Moose   Opossum   Porcupine   Rabbit

Raccoon   Skunk   Squirrel   Wolf   Woodchuck

Harvest Your Own Clay

Age: 3+

- Shovel or trowel
- Clay-rich soil
- 2 buckets
- Strainer or mesh
- Stick (optional)
- Old T-shirt or pillowcase

What kid doesn't love playing with clay? I'll never forget my first time in the Sonoran Desert in Arizona. As I walked beside towering saguaro cacti, something out of place caught my eye. It was an ornate broken piece of ancient pottery that had been made from processed desert clay beds hundreds of years ago by the Hohokam People in that region. This incredible relic now sits on my desk at home and is the inspiration behind sharing this project.

Clay was used by First Nations People to make pots, plates, storage vessels, spoons, whistles, ammunition for throwing slings, and countless types of sculptures. It is still used extensively today by artists, potters, engineers, and many others. What's interesting is that clay has not changed much in thousands of years. It is still harvested from the earth in much the same way it always has been.

Extracting clay particles from soil to create moldable clay for making pottery or sculptures is one of the most magical experiences in the outdoors. Working with clay is a great sensory activity for children. It encourages them to work with their hands and be creative. It also gives them permission to get dirty, which is simply good for a kid's soul.

Finding and processing good clay is a remarkably interesting series of steps, which are outlined in the following project. Please note this project can take up to 24 hours to complete due to the draining time. Prepare to get a little muddy, work with your hands, and be creative! You are about to embark on one of the most rewarding afternoons of your life.

INSTRUCTIONS

Step 1: The first step is to find some clay-rich soil. This is a great opportunity to go on a hike! The best place to look for clay-rich soil is in riverbeds and creek bottoms. In general, clay and clay-rich soil are beneath the top layers of earthy soil where plants are growing, so it is easiest to find in places where a creek or river carves down through the ground. In dry conditions and desert regions, you can often recognize clay-rich soil as cracked plates in the shallows of a dried-up riverbed. In this photo, you can see the clay-rich soil right at the water level and also all along the bottom of the creek. Once you find it, use your shovel to dig some up and put some in your bucket to take home.

Step 2: Natural-found clay contains impurities. This can include plants, sticks, bugs, sand, and rock. These impurities must be removed before it can be used to make pottery. While there are several ways to do this, my favorite is the wet extraction method. Start by filling the bucket with your clay-rich soil almost full with water. Place a second empty bucket with your strainer on top nearby.

Step 3: Break up the clay-rich soil in the water as much as you can with your hands. Then stir the clay with a stick or the handle of your shovel. This process will separate the clay particles from the sand and rock. Clay is made from very fine particles that will mix with the water and create a muddy slurry. The little rocks and sand will fall to the bottom, and the clay particles will remain suspended in the water. Let the mixture settle for 5 minutes.

Step 4: Pour the clay slurry through the strainer and into the clean bucket. The strainer will catch a lot of impurities. As you get to the bottom you will see everything that is not clay such as sand and rocks. Stop pouring when you see this material because you need

to discard it. Repeat this process several times until there is very little sand and gravel left over.

Step 5: Now that all (or most) of the non-clay rocks and materials have been removed, you'll be left with a mixture composed primarily of water and floating clay particles. Pour off the water in order to keep just the clay. The best way I've found to do this is to strain the water through fabric. In this example, I'm using a cotton T-shirt with the bottom knotted off and the stir stick through the sleeves as a makeshift hanger that can be tied and hung from a branch. A pillowcase also works well for this. Once you've poured the mixture into your fabric, let this stand and drip until the water is gone. It can take up to 24 hours—it is surprising how long it takes for the water to seep through the fabric and away from the clay. As the water drips and evaporates away, you will be left with workable clay!

PARENT'S GUIDE

Tips to Improve Engagement

- The obvious way to boost engagement with this project is to use the clay to sculpt something. My kids love making "pinch pots." These are simply small pots that are made by pinching the rim to shape with your fingers. They are quick, simple, and intuitive to make. You can let these pots dry and harden to make semi-durable earthenware or sculptures.

- One fun activity when working with clay is to make pictographs. Pictographs are simply symbols or drawings that represent a word or story. Ancient pictographs can still be found on rocks and in caves all throughout the American Southwest. When your kids' hands are wet with clay, they can make pictographs on paper, a cardboard box, a backyard fence, or the wall of a garden shed.

Tips for Storing Clay

- Clay has an infinite shelf life. Even if it dries out, all you have to do is add water and mix it back up to make it workable again. For short-term storage, simply put your clay in a plastic bag and twist the top tightly. It will retain moisture for several weeks like this when kept in a cool, dry area.

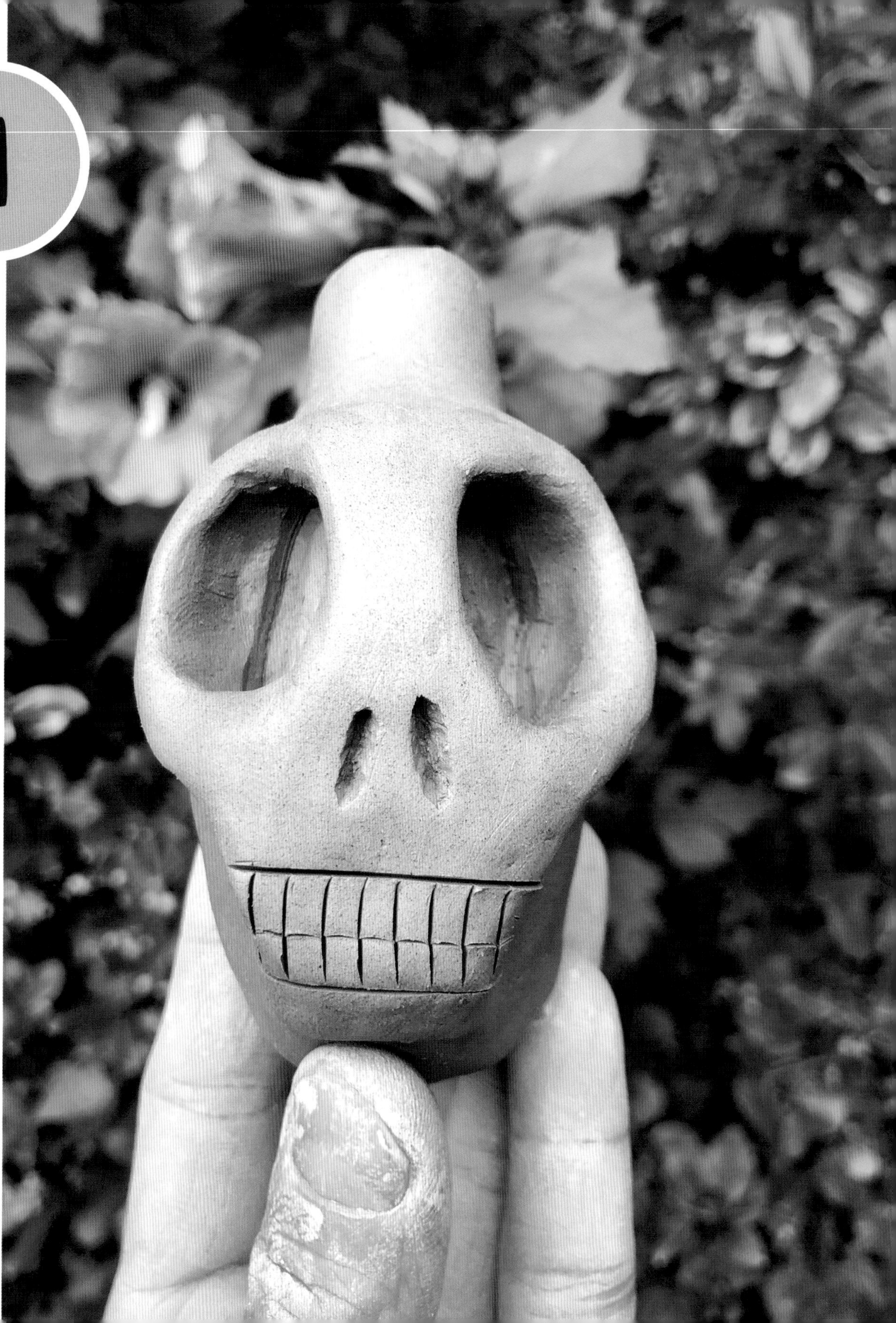

Project 4

Make an Aztec Clay Whistle

Age: 5+

MATERIALS NEEDED

- 1 cup clay
- Small spoon or butter knife
- No. 2 pencil

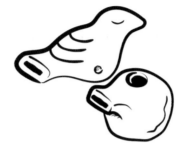

The Aztec culture is rich in ceremony and tradition. The Aztecs lived in central and southern Mexico from the fourteenth to sixteenth centuries and are well known for their ornate monuments and spectacular empire remains.

Skull imagery seems to be synonymous with ancient Aztec culture. Adorning stone tablets, monuments, and everything in between, the symbol of the human skull was a prominent symbol in Aztec culture. A skull also adorned the outside of what is now referred to as the Aztec death whistle.

Aztec death whistles were made from clay. They were essentially a unique clay whistle body enveloped in a molded clay skull, which made an eerie wailing sound when blown. Although no one knows for sure, some hypothesize that these whistles may have been blown by the hundreds along jungle hillsides by Aztec warriors before battle to drive fear into the hearts, minds, and souls of their enemies. If so, I bet it worked!

While I think that use of these whistles as a means of intimidation before war is very interesting, I'm more impressed with the notion of crafting a whistle from clay, especially since you now know how to find and process your own clay in the wild (see the previous project). A signal whistle of any kind is just as good at getting the attention of would-be rescuers as it is at intimidating one's enemy. In this tutorial, you'll learn how to make your very own clay Aztec death whistle to be used for survival or fun.

INSTRUCTIONS

Step 1: The whistle body is what's responsible for making the sound. Theoretically, once you've made that, you'll have a usable survival whistle. The decorative skull is just for show. Start by forming a solid ball of clay a little bit larger than a golf ball.

Step 2: Cut the clay ball through the middle into two equal halves. Take care not to smash the ball in this process. Use your small spoon or knife to hollow out each half.

Step 3: Now it's time to fit the two halves back together so that you have a hollow ball. Spread a mixture of clay and water (called slip) over the edges and press the two halves back together. The slip will act as a glue. Smooth over the seam with your fingers and a little more slip. At this point you should have a hollow ball a little larger than a golf ball. (Note: I have not yet smoothed the seam on the hollow clay ball in this photo.)

Step 4: Grab the clay that you hollowed out of the two ball halves. You're going to use this to form the mouthpiece. Roll the clay to form a shape about the size of a small sausage (2 inches by 3 inches).

Step 5: Use the pencil to drill a hole all the way through the mouthpiece you just formed. Take your time to not deform the shape. Next, use your pencil to create a hole anywhere in your hollow ball that's just a little bigger in diameter than the pencil. Take a minute to tidy up and smooth all the edges inside and out well. You don't want little bits of clay or jagged edges around the hole because this will affect airflow.

Step 6: Place the hollow ball up against your chin with the carved hole near your lips. Blow a tight stream of air at an angle down into the hole. You may have to make minor adjustments, but it's important that you get it to

whistle. When you do, make a mental note of how your mouth is positioned. After you've done this, it's time to place the mouthpiece so that when you blow it, a whistle noise is made like when you had the hollow ball up to your mouth. The only difference is that the mouthpiece is channeling the air. The angle must be perfect. This will require trial and error, but continually try blowing through the mouthpiece at different angles and make tweaks until you re-create the whistle sound. Once you've found the correct placement for the mouthpiece, use a little extra clay to form a supporting structure to hold the mouthpiece in place. Be sure to continuously blow through the mouthpiece to make sure you haven't moved it from the sweet spot. Finish with more clay to make sure the mouthpiece isn't going to move.

6a

6b

PARENT'S GUIDE

Tips to Improve Engagement

- If you like to make the skull portion of this Aztec death whistle, I have created a full step-by-step tutorial that you can download at the online resource page for this book here: CreekStewart.com/FamilyGuide. Not a fan of skulls? An Aztec death whistle can just as easily be transformed into a cute teddy bear whistle, a panda whistle, or any other animal for that matter.

- Rumor has it that the Aztecs used these types of whistles because they made a creepy sound like a human wailing or screaming. Have a death whistle competition to see who can make the creepiest and scariest sound. Would it intimidate you if you heard hundreds of them sounding like this in a dark forest before battle?

- Learn how to signal for rescue! The universal signal for distress is three equally spaced whistle blasts repeated over and over five seconds in between each set of three. Have your children remember this and practice it just in case.

- Has this whistle project awakened an inner whistle-making passion in your young adventurer? If so, I would like to invite to you take my Online Survival Whistle-Making Course for *free*. You can find the link here: CreekStewart.com/FamilyGuide. In this course I teach how to make nine different whistles out of trash or common household items. Use the code FAMILYGUIDE for a 100 percent discount.

Paint Gnome Rocks

Age: 3+

MATERIALS NEEDED

- Gnome-shaped rocks
- Paint, variety of colors
- Small paintbrushes
- Black marker

Gnomes spark the magical curiosity in every child. The name itself is derived from a latin word meaning "earth dweller." Clay gnomes were popularized in Germany as early as the 1800s and were placed in the corners of gardens and yards for good luck and mystical protection. Since then, they have spread all over the world and even into mainstream cartoons, movies, T-shirts, and more. Their appeal is universal, especially to children.

Armed with paints and brushes, your kids can quickly transform found rocks into woodland gnomes. Within a few minutes, entire villages of colorful, bearded gnomes can be watching over the backyard or garden. Or they can be placed strategically along local hiking trails to bring a smile to all who pass by. They also make great gifts! Painting gnomes will give your children an opportunity to express their individuality. And finding the perfect "gnome rock" is great outdoor fun in itself.

Painting gnome rocks is a great excuse to stretch your legs and get outside. Head to a rocky creek or gravelly trail to hunt for a pocketful of stones that are destined to be brought to life with a few strokes of the artist's brush. If your kids are like mine, one gnome is never enough, and the yard is not safe without at least one hundred standing watch!

INSTRUCTIONS

Step 1: Making gnome rocks begins with a search for the perfect rock. All gnomes have a floppy, cone-shaped hat and healthy beard, so you're looking for a rock that has somewhat of a triangular shape. The top part is the hat, and the bottom is the beard.

Step 2: Start by painting an oval nose in the middle of the rock as shown. Different skin tones can be made by mixing red, yellow, white, and blue. Blue is used for darker skin tones.

Step 3: Time to make the hat. Paint the pointed top of your rock in your hat color of choice. Bringing the bottom of the hat up and over the nose as shown gives a good effect when finished.

Step 4: Paint everything below the nose and hat white to create the beard.

Step 5: When the paint has dried, use a black marker to outline the nose and create the cuff of the hat as shown. If you're feeling extra creative, you can draw in beard details as well.

PARENT'S GUIDE

Tips to Improve Engagement

- When searching for gnome rocks, you will inevitably hear your child shout, "This rock looks like a _____." Whether it's a ninja, ice-cream cone, dog, or unicorn, tell them to bring it along. Painting gnomes gets kids in a headspace of imaginative creativity. Now is a great time to pull out the differently shaped rocks and bring them to life as well. After this activity, rocks will never be the same again. They are simply little bland canvases waiting to be brought alive with color and faces.

- After the gnomes are done, it's time for a very special gnome-hiding hike. This is basically the opposite of an Easter egg hunt. Go to a local park and secretly hide gnomes in wilderness nooks and cracks to surprise and bring a smile to the next person that happens by. Our family finds little treasures like these in the parks near our home and my kids absolutely love taking them. They talk about how they got there and who might have made them with a sense of awe and wonder. Then, we hide them again for others to find.

Weave a Wildflower Crown

Age: 3+

MATERIALS NEEDED

- 3 (36-inch) leather laces
- Scissors or pocketknife (optional)
- Various wildflowers

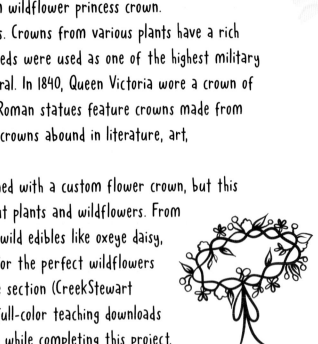

One of my wife's favorite childhood memories is when she, her sister, her mother, and her grandmother would make wildflower princess crowns in the summer. It's a tradition she now does with our daughter. I don't know that anything else makes my daughter's eyes light up like being fitted with a custom wildflower princess crown.

But wilderness-inspired crowns aren't just for girls. Crowns from various plants have a rich history. Crowns made from wildflowers, grass, and weeds were used as one of the highest military honors in ancient Rome, bestowed to a victorious general. In 1840, Queen Victoria wore a crown of orange blossoms on her wedding day. Both Greek and Roman statues feature crowns made from leaves and plant sprigs. Historical instances of flower crowns abound in literature, art, and sculpture.

The kids will love the special feeling of being adorned with a custom flower crown, but this project is also a great opportunity to teach them about plants and wildflowers. From plants to stay away from like poison ivy to beneficial wild edibles like oxeye daisy, there are many great lessons to teach when hunting for the perfect wildflowers to decorate your crowns. Check out the Parent's Guide section (CreekStewart .com/FamilyGuide) where I have made available some full-color teaching downloads for several flowering plants you may cross paths with while completing this project.

INSTRUCTIONS

Step 1: Leather lacing can be found in the leather-working aisle of your local craft store. Tie the ends of the three leather laces together using an overhand knot.

Step 2: Braid the laces in a loose braid using a standard three-strand braid. This is the same braid commonly used to braid hair. The small gaps in the braid are for wildflower stems later.

Step 3: Continue until the braid is long enough to fit around the head of the person it is being made for, then knot the end with an overhand knot.

Step 4: Now pull the first knot through the braid just before the last knot as a clasp. You can trim the loose leather laces or leave them hanging. The size can easily be adjusted by moving the knot up and down the braid.

Step 5: Cut the wildflowers, leaving 2–3 inches of stem on each. Insert the stems through the leather braid toward the middle as shown. Do this around the entire perimeter of the crown. Add as few or as many as you wish!

PARENT'S GUIDE

A Note about Conservation

- Emphasize to your kids the importance of not carelessly stripping all of the flowers from one plant (one here and there is okay). Explain that flowers are how plants attract pollinators, such as bees, for producing fruits and seeds. Choose your wildflowers sparingly from any given area.

Safety Notes

- While handling wildflowers in most cases is very safe, there are several flowers that I'd suggest staying away from, such as poison hemlock and wild parsnip. Poison hemlock is one of the deadliest plants in North America, and the sap from wild parsnip reacts with the sun to cause a nasty rash that can last for months. For these reasons and more, I would apply similar rules to this activity that I apply to harvesting wild edible plants. Harvest only the flowers that you know.

Tips to Improve Engagement

- This project is just as much fun in cold weather as it is in warm weather. Instead of flowers, you'll be looking for bristly foxtail grasses, green sprigs of juniper or cedar, pine needles, and fluffy seed pods. In my opinion, a winter version of the flower crown is just as unique and ornate.

- Visit the online resource page for this book at CreekStewart.com/FamilyGuide to download several full-color identification sheets that I've created for a variety of wildflowers that you might come across when building flower crowns. Use these guides to learn about different flowers on your hikes.

CHAPTER 3

FUN AND GAMES

If there was ever a place for fun and games, it is outside. While inside the home is safe and familiar, every kid knows that outside is where the real adventures are to be had. This chapter puts together a list of outdoor projects that will capture the adventurous spirit of any child.

My goal is to introduce you and your kids to a variety of new skills, and even unexplored natural materials. I specifically chose projects in hopes that they would be first-time experiences for everyone. For example, very few people have ever woven a duck decoy from dried cattail leaves or made a shepherd's sling to throw tennis balls.

The materials needed to accomplish these projects are minimal. With Mother Nature as the arena for play, the truth is that not much else is needed. Many have been wired to believe that fun can only be had with expensive toys, fast-paced videos, elaborate plans, or over-the-top activities. This is not true. The key is doing things together. Your time is the most important thing you can give your children. There is no substitute for your authentic engagement as a parent in these activities, so remember what it was like to be a kid, and have some fun!

Leaf Rubbing Journal

Age: 5+

> **MATERIALS NEEDED**
>
> - Printed journal pages (or blank 8½-inch by 11-inch white paper)
> - Scissors
> - Hole punch
> - Rubber band
> - Small stick (8 inches long by about ¼ inch in diameter)
> - Leaves (that you'll find on your hike)
> - Crayons, paper labels removed

Nature journaling is not only an educational opportunity but it also allows children to experience and record nature while creating something unique. There are many different types of nature journaling, from writing down what one sees and hears to sketching natural items. For children, one of the best nature journals is one made of leaf rubbings. Leaf rubbing is part art and part science!

Not only can your child record a huge variety of tree leaves but it is also a fantastic way to learn about botanical leaf features and different species of trees. Tree identification is a life skill worth learning. My grandpa used to say that every good woodsman or woodswoman knows their trees. Consider taking your leaf rubbing journals on vacations to record tree leaves that you don't find in your area. Over time you will create quite an impressive record and knowledge base of leaf types and tree species.

The local park or green space is the perfect spot to start your leaf rubbing adventure. It is a very noninvasive activity that requires simple materials and is fun for all ages. Be sure to download the printable Leaf Rubbing Journal I've created for you, which includes fill-in-the-blank spaces for your child's name, tree species, and more. Creating this small journal is a fun project in itself and prepares you for the adventure ahead!

INSTRUCTIONS

Step 1: Start by printing the Leaf Rubbing Journal I've created for you at the online resource page for this book at CreekStewart.com/FamilyGuide. Print the cover page and several of the interior leaf rubbing pages. Fold the cover page in half and then cut the other pages along the cut line in the middle.

Step 2: Insert the interior pages into the folded cover page and punch a hole 1 inch from the top and bottom (about ½ inch in from the spine) as shown. If you don't have a hole punch, you can also just staple the pages together on the fold line if you wish and skip Step 3.

Step 3: While holding the stick along the folded edge of the front cover, feed one end of the rubber band up through the top hole and around the end of the stick. Then feed the other end of the rubber band up through the bottom hole and around the other end of your stick. This adds a natural element to the journal and helps hold the pages together.

Step 4: Now it's time to go for a hike to collect some leaves! Place a leaf underneath one of the pages and use a crayon turned on its side to rub over the leaf. The raised parts of the leaf and the edges will show darker, and a permanent record of the leaf will be created on the page. Repeat this process using different leaves on each page of the journal to fill it up!

Step 5: Fill in the details! Be sure to use the back cover of the journal as a guide to learn about common leaf shapes found in nature!

PARENT'S GUIDE

Safety Notes

- While there aren't any poisonous trees to be concerned about when leaf rubbing, be wary of any vines that may be growing on trees. Poison ivy (mainly eastern United States) and poison oak (mainly western United States) are common vines that will grow up and around the trunks of trees.

Tips to Improve Engagement

- Leaf rubbing is a very active project and great for groups. Bringing along a few friends always helps spike engagement in activities like this. Whether it's cousins or classmates, seeing who can create the largest collection of rubbings in a given amount of time is a good, healthy competition. Then a follow-up game of "Guess That Tree" based on leaf rubbings is a good way to teach tree identification skills in a creative way.

- Plant a tree! Did you know that most state Department of Natural Resources offices will allow you to order tree seedlings at no to very little cost? Wrapping up an afternoon of leaf rubbing with a tree planting ceremony is a great way to teach children about giving back to future generations.

- A note about conservation: Emphasize the importance of not carelessly stripping leaves from any tree (one here and there is okay). Explain that the leaves are how the tree gathers sunlight to make energy for food production. The tree will starve without its leaves!

Make a Bull-Roarer

Age: 7+

A bull-roarer, also known as a groaning stick and wolf-scare, is a carved piece of wood tied to a short piece of cord. When swung overhead in circles, it emits an incredibly unique low-frequency buzzing noise and has a history deeply rooted in medicinal and spiritual practices. This low-frequency noise can travel for miles.

MATERIALS NEEDED

- Marker
- Paint stirring stick
- Pocketknife or scissors
- 36-inch piece butcher's twine

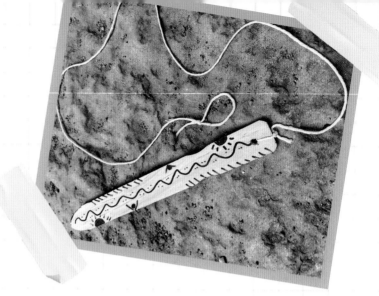

Bull-roarer history is rich in a variety of ceremonial uses, and historical writings are peppered with references of the bull-roarer serving as a long-distance communication device, a tribal alarm system, and a tool to flush out or scare animals and birds for hunting. Regardless of use, it is a most intriguing primitive tool. In fact, the bull-roarer was utilized in completely unrelated primitive cultures all over the globe, which is itself a marvel.

Some refer to the bull-roarer as the first cell phone—a tool to send messages over long distances. How cool is that?! The idea that a long-range message-delivering communication tool can be carved, assembled, and deployed using just a stick and a piece of cordage is nothing short of amazing. Indigenous cultures used certain noise patterns to communicate unique messages, like how Morse code is used in modern times.

How does it work? As you spin the bull-roarer overhead, the wooden paddle meets the resistance of the air and begins to twist and vibrate. It is this fast vibration that creates low-pitched buzzing. The pitch of the sound can be changed up or down by the speed in which you spin the bull-roarer overhead.

So grab a free paint stick from your local hardware store and tell your kids you're going to all head outside and make the world's first cell phone. That will certainly get their attention!

INSTRUCTIONS

Step 1: Use the marker to draw a rounded tip toward the last quarter of the paint stick. The exact location doesn't matter.

Step 2: Using a pocketknife or scissors, carefully carve away the tip of the paint stick past the curved line drawn in Step 1. Paint sticks are prone to splitting so carving away from the bull-roarer body and toward the tip will prevent you from potentially splitting your bull-roarer.

Step 3: Using the point of the pocketknife, carefully twist a hole in the bottom portion of the paint stick as shown. This should be roughly $\frac{1}{2}$ inch from the end and right in the middle. To prevent the stick from splitting, twist the knife a few times on one side and then switch to the other side to twist a few times. Alternate sides until a hole is all the way through. Be sure to do this on a hard surface and not over your lap or hand.

Step 4: Tie one end of the butcher's twine through the hole using a double half hitch knot (shown) or simply two to three overhand knots. *Important: Tie a final overhand knot on the short tail. This small knot will prevent the tail from slipping through during spinning.*

Step 5: Tie an overhand finger loop at the other end of the twine.

Step 6: To use the bull-roarer, put the loop over the index or middle finger of your dominant hand. Then, twist the wooden paint stick until the twine begins to kink (usually at least fifty twists). Once the rope kinks, let go of the paint stick and swing it as fast as you can over your head. You should hear low-frequency buzzing almost immediately.

PARENT'S GUIDE

Safety Notes

- A bull-roarer can be made without any carving. The carved rounded tip is completely optional and does not affect performance. I like to do it in my courses because it adds another hands-on layer to what is otherwise a very short project.

- If you choose to use a pocketknife and do some carving, please read my wood carving safety tips under the project titled "Carve an Old Man Face in a Bar of Soap" in this chapter.

- Don't use bull-roarers indoors.

- Keep at least a 10-foot distance from anyone who is spinning a bull-roarer just in case the loop slips off their finger or the wooden stick comes off.

- For first-time bull-roarer users, safety glasses aren't a bad idea. While I've never had a user hit themselves in the face, it is technically possible. Prevention is the best cure!

Tips to Improve Engagement

- Have your kids decorate their bull-roarers. Personalizing the bull-roarer gives them an opportunity to be creative. Encourage them to draw pictograph-type drawings of animals or landscapes, or intricate designs. Markers or paints work well for this.

- Another great way to improve engagement is to place two bull-roarer users on opposite sides of a house or obstruction and have them "talk" to each other. One person will spin, then stop and wait for the other person to do the same. Who needs walkie-talkies when you have bull-roarers?

Weave a Cattail Duck Decoy

Age: 5+

In the early twentieth century, eleven duck decoys made from tule (pronounced TOO-lee) were discovered inside Lovelock Cave in Nevada during an archeological dig. They were made and used by the Northern Paiute and cultures before them to attract and hunt a huge variety of waterfowl that were attracted to the resource-rich waters of the Great Basin area.

Cattail leaves, plant material similar to tule, are used for weaving. Cattails can be found in nearly every part of the world except for the Arctic. I've even spotted cattail plants at watering holes in the Sonoran Desert. Cattails grow from underground rhizomes and will regrow any leaves you use for crafting, so don't worry about hurting the plant. And they typically grow in dense stands of many hundreds and thousands. Cattails will always be found near water or ditches. They grow long green swordlike leaves. But the telltale feature to look for is the corncob-like seed head that grows atop a central stalk. It starts green in spring and turns brown and fluffy toward the end of summer and fall.

It's best to cut the cattails when the leaves are green and at their peak of maturity—typically in July and August. Then separate the leaves to increase airflow and allow them to dry directly in the sun for several days to a couple of weeks, depending on the conditions. You can place them on pretty much any surface, but ideal spots are on a table, deck, or back porch. Be sure to put them up inside if it rains. You'll want to let them dry until they reach a nice tan color. Four to six handfuls of dried cattail leaves will be required to make one duck decoy.

Once dry, cattail leaves are brittle. Ironically, they need to be soaked for about 30 minutes or so to ready them for weaving, like how basketmaking materials need to be soaked before making baskets. The exterior of wetted cattail leaves will feel velvety to the touch, and it's amazing how much more durable and pliable they become when they've been soaked before use. They can be sprayed with a garden hose in the yard several times or soaked in the bathtub or a pond for about 30 minutes.

INSTRUCTIONS

Step 1: Soak the dried cattail leaves for about 30 minutes to ready them for weaving. In this photo I am soaking some at the edge of a pond, weighted down with rocks.

Step 2: Start by taking two of your best cattail blades that are the thickest and at least 30–36 inches long. Place them directly together with the cut ends on the same side and fold them in half. Then fold the folded tip down about 4–5 inches. This will be the beak portion of the duck.

Step 3: Use cattail leaves to wrap around the head and neck area. The goal here is to start filling out and shaping the head and forehead of the duck. When you reach the end of a leaf, simply tuck it under the previous one and pull tight. (Do this for all leaf ends throughout the entire project.) Continue wrapping leaves to make a duck head shape as shown.

Step 4: The body is made from two *big* handfuls of cattail leaves. One handful should have all the cut ends aligned and facing LEFT and the other should have all the cut ends aligned and facing RIGHT. Combine these two handfuls of leaves into one bundle, as shown, and wrap strong cattail leaves around the bundle in the middle. Then bend the entire bundle across your knee to fold it in half.

Step 5: Insert the neck of the duck head into the folded middle of the bundle and tie the two sides of the bundle tightly together with twisted cattail leaves to pinch and hold the duck head into place. You can also use leaves to tie and secure the head if desired.

PARENT'S GUIDE

Safety Notes

- While there are some plants that resemble the cattail, including the poisonous wild iris, none have the telltale corncob-like fluffy seed head. In every stand of cattails, no matter the season, there will be fluffy seed heads from the previous season's cattail plants. Look for these seed heads when identifying and harvesting the cattail. The best time for harvest is July and August. The seed heads will be unmistakable at this time.

- It is very important to separate the individual leaves before drying them. If you don't, the leaves will mold, and you don't want to be breathing that in while working with them. You'll also want to move the leaves around over the drying period to allow airflow all around each leaf.

Tips for Improving Engagement

- The first thing every child will want to do when they make a cattail duck decoy is to see if it floats. This is a perfect reason to head to the local park, pond, or creek and give them a try. Some will float perfectly, some will turn upside down, some will turn sideways, but it is always a good time to see the craft in action. Afterward, they make great gifts or decorations in the house.

- Making cattail duck decoys can take a couple of hours. For kids with shorter attention spans, there are tons of other uses for cattails as well. All cattail projects begin with the same drying and wetting process as described earlier. One skill in particular that I always teach when working with cattails is three-strand braiding. This is the same braid that you would use to braid hair. When braided together, cattail leaves make extraordinary rope. See who can win a cattail rope tug-of-war.

Make a Tennis Ball Shepherd's Sling

Age: 7+

MATERIALS NEEDED

- Sling template
- 5-inch by 10-inch piece leather or canvas
- Scissors
- 550 paracord
- Marker

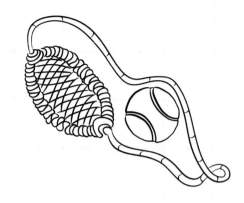

Shepherd's slings make appearances in many historical texts, drawings, carvings, and stories. From King Tut's tomb in Egypt to the cave excavations in the western United States, throwing slings have been utilized worldwide. Shepherd's slings were used to protect sheep from wolves, to hunt small game, and as a toy for throwing games and target practice. One of the most famous accounts of the sling's use was in the biblical account of David and Goliath.

In this tutorial you'll learn how to make a fantastic sling to throw tennis balls. This will be especially useful for children with dogs that like to play catch! Using a shepherd's sling is not only a fun and unique activity but also great exercise. Like any throwing sport, mastering the sling requires practice, dedication, and focus. These are all great character traits to develop in any child.

No child will ever forget the moment they make their first dead-on target hit with a shepherd's sling. The sling is a tool owned by very few people in the world, and the skill to use one is even rarer. Each sling is custom-made per the user's body measurements, so it will be a one of a kind. Join the sling club today by building your own using the steps that follow here!

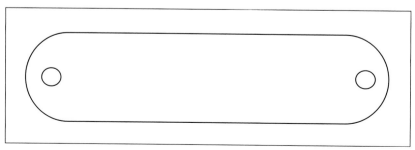

Copy template at 200%

INSTRUCTIONS

Step 1: Download and print the custom sling pouch template at CreekStewart.com/FamilyGuide and trace it in two places on your leather or canvas. If you're using leather, make sure it is thin and flexible, not thick and stiff.

Step 2: Cut out the two-piece sling pouch using scissors.

Step 3: Cut two pieces of 550 paracord that are the length of the distance from your fingertips to the center of your chest.

Step 4: Tie one end of each strand through the holes on each side of the pouches using a double half hitch knot (shown). Tie an overhand knot on the short end to prevent the knot from coming undone. This is called a stopper knot to prevent the tail from slipping through while in use.

Step 5: Note how the two pouch pieces are overlapping. Each piece has one side that is on top and the other side on bottom.

Step 6: Tie a small overhand loop on the end of one of the long cords and an overhand knot on the end of the other one. (An overhand loop is simply an overhand knot tied with the string doubled over so that it creates a fixed loop.) The loop goes on the middle finger of the dominant throwing hand and the knot on the other strand is pinched between the index finger and thumb. When held up, each side of the sling should be equal with the pouch centered below. If not, adjust knots on the end of the strands accordingly.

PARENT'S GUIDE

Safety Notes

- While using tennis balls as projectiles makes them no more dangerous than playing tennis, there are still a few safety notes to communicate to your children. First is to only use tennis balls as projectiles. These are reasonably soft and fun to use. Second, make sure everyone keeps a safe distance from active slingers. Using a sling requires slinging the tennis ball-filled pouch in circles above your head. Not only can someone get hit during this process but oftentimes the tennis ball will fly out in any direction—especially when first learning how to sling. A distance of at least 10 to 15 feet from active slingers is advised.

How to Use a Sling

- While there are many different slinging techniques, I prefer the one that involves slinging the sling over your head. First, the overhand loop should go over the middle finger on your dominant hand. The overhand knot at the end of the other cord should be pinched between the index finger and thumb. Next, slightly spread apart the pouch pieces and place a tennis ball inside. Then swing the sling overhead two times. On the return of the second swing, release the knot between the thumb and index finger; the force of the swing will launch the tennis ball forward. Because this is better seen than read, I have filmed a short tutorial video where I teach this technique. You can watch that video at the online resource link at CreekStewart.com/FamilyGuide.

Attract Birds with a Pine Cone Bird Feeder

Age: 3+

MATERIALS NEEDED

- 2 cups peanut butter
- Butter knife or spoon
- Dried pine cone
- Long plastic pan or tray
- Birdseed
- 18 inches string

It is important to help foster an authentic connection between our children and nature. Doing so helps them to become personally invested in protecting and preserving it. In addition, numerous studies have also shown that peaceful activities like bird-watching can reduce anxiety and stress in people of all ages. Watching birds is calming and a fantastic way for kids to learn about some of the more than seventeen thousand species of birds in the world.

Millions of people each year participate in the hobby of bird-watching. A friend of mine, Alan Baczkiewicz, was introduced to birding by his father at a young age, and it is now a hobby that has become a big part of his life, even in adulthood. In fact, he is the author of a book on the subject titled *The Backyard Bird Sanctuary*. My point in telling you this is that a simple introduction to an outdoor activity could change a child's life. I earned my Wilderness Survival merit badge as a young Boy Scout, and it planted a seed that would grow into a very rewarding career in outdoor skills training, and eventually this book. Plant as many outdoor seeds into young people as possible. You never know which ones will take root!

The first step for any beginning birder is to set up a backyard or back patio bird feeder to attract local species of our feathered friends. But before you go out and spend money on a store-bought one, consider spending some time with your kiddos making this one from a pine cone, some peanut butter, and birdseed. This is an especially great activity in the winter when food is scarcer for birds and outdoor activities are scarcer for children.

INSTRUCTIONS

Step 1: Smear peanut butter between the scales of the pine cone.

Step 2: Roll the peanut butter–covered pine cone in birdseed or use your hand to pack birdseed all over it. This is best done in a long plastic tray or pan, but I have yet to find a way of preventing a mess with my kids.

Step 3: Tie on a loop of string for hanging outside.

PARENT'S GUIDE

Safety Notes

- Be aware of any peanut allergies.

Tips to Improve Engagement

- Although making a peanut-buttery pine cone mess is a great time, the real fun starts when this improvised bird feeder is hung up. Within hours, curious feathered friends will be pecking their choice of seed kernels from between the sticky peanut butter-filled pine cone scales. A great way to keep kids engaged in this project is to keep a bird visiting log where you record various observations about each bird, including a drawing. You'll be surprised at the number of different birds your young one will record in just a few weeks. Before long they will have a book of their own! To help jump-start this journal, I have created a free printable download that you can use. It is available at the online resource page for this book at CreekStewart.com/FamilyGuide. There is also a template toward the end of this book that will work well as a bird-watching journal.

- If bird-watching seems to be an activity that your child enjoys, a bird identification guide can go a long way to building their knowledge base and helping them learn the language surrounding bird-watching. Every hobby has a "language," and bird-watching is no different. A good guide to reference is the natural next step to developing this hobby. Ones I recommend for kids are the *National Geographic Kids Bird Guide of North America* and *The Backyard Bird Sanctuary* by my friend Alan Baczkiewicz.

- Don't overlook that going on a pine cone hunt is a great start to this activity! Kids love looking for nature treasures. While different pine trees produce different sizes and shapes of cones, nearly all will work. You can find dried pine cones on the ground beneath the trees. A great place to look for these is local parks, green spaces, and hiking trails. No special preparation is required besides being dry. If they are wet when you find them, just place them in a window sill for a couple days and they'll dry.

Carve an Old Man Face in a Bar of Soap

Age: 7+

MATERIALS NEEDED

- Bar of soap
- Pocketknife
- Black marker

Pocketknife handling skills are quickly becoming a lost art. Learning how to safely and properly use a pocketknife is an essential life skill. Working with a pocketknife teaches children many valuable lessons, including hand-eye coordination. It also opens an entirely new world of creative opportunities and personal responsibilities.

Children as young as seven years old can be taught to safely use a pocketknife with simple carving projects like this one. Soap is the perfect medium for beginning carvers. It is easy to carve and shows results very quickly. Carving a simple face in a bar of soap as shown in this project will teach a child many different pocketknife handling skills.

In addition to teaching how to safely use a pocketknife, carving helps a child to focus on a very specific task. In this day and age of constant distractions, moments of focus are a real treasure. For this reason, carving is one of my favorite activities to do with my son. There is a risk of injury that oftentimes adds to the intensity of focus. No one wants to get cut!

To transform soap from a boring block into a face, figurine, or shape inspires creativity and brings a true sense of accomplishment. Permission to use a pocketknife feels like a rite of passage to a child. For that reason, carving sessions foster a sense of pride and confidence that many other types of projects do not. In addition, carving teaches respect for one's tools. Cleaning and proper storage should be a part of every whittling project.

INSTRUCTIONS

Step 1: Shave the front of your soap flat and use the marker to draw on a cross with drooping arms and a small triangle underneath. These lines will be your carving guide throughout the project. The drooping arms are the brow lines, and the triangle is the nose.

Step 2: Carve away some soap under the brow lines and around the nose. Also carve a little bit away from underneath the nose all the way to the bottom of the bar of soap.

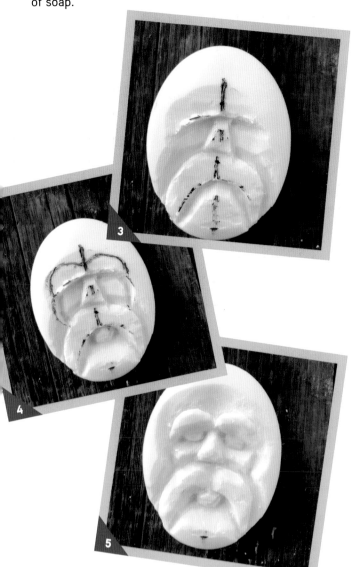

Step 3: Use the marker to redraw the centerline and draw in a mustache. After you have the mustache drawn on, use the knife to carve some relief outside of that line. The best technique for this is to use the pocketknife to make an outline ¼ inch deep in the soap along the mustache line and then carve into that cut line from outside the mustache. This will give the mustache a raised effect.

Step 4: Draw on some eyebrows. Also, use the knife to carve some definition for the cheekbones and the lower lip.

Step 5: Carve around the eyebrows to make them pop, and outline the eyes with relief cuts. Relief cuts are made by making an outline ¼ inch deep in the soap along the eyebrow lines and then carving into that cut line from outside the eyebrow. Do your best to round off all straight edges around the eyebrows and mustache. Then finish with any minor details you'd like in order to personalize the face!

PARENT'S GUIDE

Safety Notes

- I am a huge advocate of kids learning how to safely use a pocketknife. I believe that safe pocketknife handling is a life skill that can start as early as seven years old for some children. But all kids are different. You'll have to use your best judgment based on your own kid's dexterity and maturity level.

- Avoid the Blood Bubble: A person's blood bubble is anywhere inside the perimeter of their own reach with a knife. This means that if another person is inside of your blood bubble, then they can get cut. Bottom line: Stay out of other people's blood bubbles and don't let them inside of yours.

- Protect the Triangle of Death: Imagine drawing a triangle between your knees and up your thighs to your groin. This is known as the Triangle of Death. It's human nature to want to carve in your lap, but it is very dangerous to do so because of the femoral artery that runs down the inside of each leg. If this artery is cut, someone can bleed to death in a matter of minutes. For this reason, you never want kids to carve in their lap. Always work on a stable work surface in a seated position, like at a picnic table.

- Cut Away from the Body: Always explain to your children that there should never be any body parts in front of the pocketknife blade, and they should never carve toward their body.

- Fold Up or Cover: When not in use, a pocketknife should always be folded back up; a fixed blade knife should always be returned to its sheath.

- Have a First Aid Kit Handy: Just as every single person who has learned to ride a bike has fallen, every single person who has learned to carve has cut themselves. Have a first aid kit on hand for minor cuts.

Tips to Improve Engagement

- Once a child has shown repeated good pocketknife handling techniques, the next step for this process is to carve faces into wood. I love doing this with hiking sticks! The best carving woods are basswood, balsa, cottonwood, willow, and tulip poplar. These are all a step up from the hardness of soap but are still considered soft woods to carve.

- At the end of each carving session, encourage your kids to thoroughly clean their knife blades so that the tool is in tip-top shape for the next time they use it. Clean knife blades with soap and water and then make sure they are thoroughly dry before putting them up so they don't rust.

CHAPTER 4

FORAGING AND FOOD

There are so many incredible memories to be had with your kids while preparing food and cooking around a campfire. Time spent cooking or foraging for food is likely where "family time" began for all humankind. It's an opportunity to teach, laugh, and tell stories. The bonus is that you get to eat as well!

This chapter includes a bit of everything when it comes to outdoor food-related projects. From building makeshift stoves and foraging for wild edibles to spiderweb nets and campfire treats, these projects are designed to not only boost confidence but also learn new skills. It is also my hope that something here will initiate the important conversation about where our food comes from. Understanding the work that goes into growing, harvesting, preparing, and cooking food can help foster a healthy appreciation for food at a young age.

For most kids, food-related activities are almost always indoors. That is precisely what makes this chapter so special. You get to challenge everything your child thinks they know about food. There is an adventure to be had by replacing the home oven with a trash tin can or foraging wild plants to make a healthful drink. Using sticks to cook bread and substituting a paper bag for a skillet will become a grand story to share at school.

One thing these projects will most certainly do is force you to slow down in what is normally a very fast-paced world. Bread or muffins can cook only so fast. Growing our own food in makeshift planters will require you to be patient. The slow 10 minutes it takes to steep a cup of fresh dandelion tea is as good for the body as the tea itself. And catching fishing bait with a net made from spiderwebs requires fortitude, focus, and patience.

Brew Dandelion Tea

Age: 7+

MATERIALS NEEDED

- 4–6 dandelion flowers
- Tea ball or spoon-style strainer
- Heatproof cup
- 16 ounces hot water
- 1 teaspoon honey or maple syrup

Most people don't realize there are dozens of wild edible plants and herbs growing in the average backyard! One of the most abundant and nutritious is the dandelion (*Taraxacum officinale*). The dandelion also happens to be one of the most familiar plants in the world. Its nutritious leaves are sold in health food stores, and a coffee substitute can even be made from the dried roots. Yet millions of dollars a year are spent on trying to eradicate it from neighborhoods and public parks. In my opinion, the best way to get rid of a dandelion is to eat it! All parts of the dandelion are edible!

In this project you'll learn how to make fresh dandelion flower tea, but you'll also be interested to know the following uses for the dandelion as well:

- The green leaves can be steamed like spinach.
- The roots can be cooked as a vegetable like carrots.
- The roots can also be dried, roasted, ground, and used as a coffee substitute (without the caffeine).
- The young buds can be sautéed as a vegetable or pickled like capers.
- The flower blooms can be batter-fried as fritters.

Truly, the dandelion is an amazing plant that has been used by people all over the world for thousands of years as both food and medicine.

While most kids love picking a dandelion after it has gone to seed, the yellow flowers make an excellent mild-flavored tea. Making tea is a great introduction foraging skill for children. And the dandelion is a great plant to start with because it is so easy to identify and has no poisonous parts. This is a good activity for kids with short attention spans: You can go from foraging to tea on the table in just about 10 minutes!

INSTRUCTIONS

Step 1: The first step is identifying a dandelion. Dandelions grow from a basal rosette of leaves. The long leaves have a broad arrowhead-shaped tip with triangular lobes along the sides that are wavy and irregular. Hollow flower stalks grow from the middle of the rosette and produce a yellow flower with dozens of ray florets that is typically 1–2 inches across. All parts of the plant have milky-white sap.

Step 2: Pluck the yellow ray florets from the rest of the dandelion flower heads. Fill a tea ball or strainer with about ¼ cup dandelion flower ray florets and place in the cup.

Step 3: Bring the water to a boil inside on the stove. Pour just-boiled water into the cup and let steep for 10 minutes. Let cool and sweeten to taste with honey or maple syrup.

PARENT'S GUIDE

Safe Foraging Notes

- Never forage edible plants from within 100 feet of roadsides. These plants are usually tainted by roadside spraying, road and ditch runoff, and vehicle exhaust and fluids.

- Never forage within 100 feet of monocrop fields like corn and soybeans. These crops are always treated with multiple passes of pesticides and herbicides, and the wind carries overspray.

- Never eat anything unless you are 100 percent positive of its identity. Use multiple plant features to positively identify any plant.

- Cross-reference wild edible plants using multiple identification guides.

Tips to Improve Engagement

- One of my favorite childhood memories is running around the yard and picking yellow dandelion blooms for my mom to make Fried Dandelion Fritters. These are simply washed dandelion blooms that where dipped in pancake batter and fried like a tiny fritter in a hot greased skillet. They are delicious. Consider taking your dandelion foraging to the next level with this easy-to-fix side dish!

- Make a field illustration! For kids who love to draw, challenge them to make a field illustration of a dandelion plant. Have them focus on the unique identifying features such as the lobed leaves, yellow blooms, hollow stems, fluffy seed heads, and basal rosette. Focusing on illustrating these features will help them to become more confident and safer foragers!

- Download Five Identification Sheet Sets: Each month I teach about a different wild edible plant through a service called Wild Edible Plant of the Month Club (WildEdiblePlantoftheMonth.com). At the online resource guide for this book, CreekStewart.com/FamilyGuide, I have provided five of these full-color identification sheet sets available for additional learning. These are five common wild edible plants that likely grow in your area. Download them for free.

Plant a Milk Carton Garden

Age: 3+

MATERIALS NEEDED

- 64-ounce empty paper milk carton
- 2 cups water
- Scissors
- Approximately 8 cups potting soil or dirt to fill carton
- 2–3 seeds each of three types of herbs
- Marker
- 3 Popsicle sticks

There are so many wonderful benefits that come from teaching your kids about gardening. Upcycled container micro-gardens like this one are the perfect way to foster a deeper connection between children and their food. In addition, many studies in the realm of ecotherapy show that working with your hands in a garden reduces stress and improves one's mood. In our disinfected world of hand sanitizer and alcohol wipes, some good quality dirt time is a refreshing reprieve for any child.

Container gardens like this one are perfect for kitchen herbs such as thyme, sage, lavender, rosemary, hyssop, lemon balm, basil, costmary, spikenard, chamomile, and pennyroyal. Herbs, as opposed to vegetables or fruits, can be harvested within just a few weeks. Quick feedback is always a good thing when working with children. Keeping a close eye on the new garden to check if it needs water is a great opportunity to teach responsibility. Growing your own food also provides a sense of independence and self-reliance. Who knows—this small project could plant the seed in your child for a love of gardening. Next year you'll be building raised beds!

INSTRUCTIONS

Step 1: Clean the inside of the milk carton by rinsing out with water. Use scissors to cut out one side of the carton. Leave the corner edges for stability.

Step 2: Fill the carton with dirt or potting soil and press in two to three of each type of seeds 1–2 inches beneath the surface. Group the like seeds together and space the different herbs evenly from one another inside of the carton. Place the milk carton garden in full sun.

Step 3: Use the marker to label each stick with the type of herb, then place each stick in the carton near that herb.

Step 4: The seeds should start sprouting in just a few days. Most kitchen herbs can be ready for harvest and enjoyed in under three weeks.

PARENT'S GUIDE

Tips to Improve Engagement

- Keep a growth chart: Using a ruler to measure weekly growth of plants is a great way to incorporate measurement and math skills by adding the inches together for weekly totals.

- See photosynthesis in action: Reading about photosynthesis in a science book is interesting, but seeing it in action is way better. In short, plants produce oxygen that we then breathe. Amazing!

- Teach the benefit of being thrifty: In addition to saving the family money by gardening at home, using a milk container is a great example of not letting things go to waste. When you're at the grocery store and see the same kinds of herbs you're growing at home, be sure to point out how much money you're saving by growing your own!

- Share the bounty: My mom was notorious for giving away some of our extra garden produce to neighbors. This was a lesson that I still remember today. It feels good to give. Encourage your child to harvest and give away some of whatever it is you decide to grow.

- Secure future harvests: The seeds from your plants can be saved to secure future harvests. Help your child clean the seeds, dry them, and store them in envelopes for next season. Encourage them to write the names and draw some images of the plants (or produce if you decide to grow more than herbs) on the envelopes.

Make a Vagabond Stove

Age: 7+

MATERIALS NEEDED

- Can punch
- No. 10 metal can, label removed (No. 10 cans are 6³/₁₆ inches wide and 7 inches high)
- Tin snips
- 2 handfuls small sticks and twigs
- Fire-building materials (see Tips to Improve Engagement for specific details)

After the Civil War in the late 1800s, many American soldiers who had no home or family took to the road in search of work. They became known as hobos or vagabonds and often hopped railcars to get from place to place. These traveling laborers packed light and used whatever resources they could gather or make on the road to survive. One of these innovations was the vagabond stove.

A vagabond stove is a simple metal cooking stove made from a trash tin can. A popular can used was the No. 10 can that was common for food packaging at the time. With a few hand tools they could whip up an improvised cooking stove on the road in about 5 minutes. This style of stove allows for a small, discreet, contained, and effective fire. You can make the same stove at home and use it to cook meals in the backyard or when you're camping. It is an ingeniously innovative way to make use of trash tin cans.

Because the cooking fire is built inside of the tin can, this is a very safe fire. Another advantage of this stove is that it doesn't require large pieces of fuel. It uses just tiny sticks and twigs that can be found in almost any environment, including a backyard. From hot dogs and s'mores to bacon and eggs, the vagabond stove is an improvised camp stove that has survived the test of time. Grab your skillet and the materials listed here and cook dinner like a vagabond tonight!

INSTRUCTIONS

Step 1: Begin by using the can punch to quickly punch out triangle-shaped holes all around the top and bottom rims of the can, about 3 inches apart. Tin can edges can be very sharp. Please see Safety Notes section that follows.

Step 2: Next, use the tin snips to cut a square door between two of the can punch holes as shown. Use the two can punch holes as pilot holes for the tin snips. Cut along the lower rim between two holes and then up about 3 inches on both sides. Then carefully fold up the tin flap by pulling up and putting pressure along the fold line with your thumbs. This opening forms the fuel door. Note the bottom of the can is on the ground in this photo. The top (cooking side) is open.

Step 3: Place your stove on a solid noncombustible surface like concrete or stone and build a small fire inside with the sticks and twigs. Simply push them in farther as they burn down. If you're not sure how to start a campfire, see the "Start a Campfire Using a Ferro Rod" activity in Chapter 5. A skillet or wok can now be placed on top for cooking. The holes along the top and bottom allow a draft of air to feed the fire with oxygen. This makes for a very efficient stove.

PARENT'S GUIDE

Safety Notes

- The cut edges of the metal can will be very sharp. Be very careful when handling the stove or cut pieces. Leather gloves are recommended. Show these sharp edges to your kids and explain that they can cause a nasty cut if not careful.

- The bottom of the stove will become scorching hot while in use. Be sure to set the stove on a safe noncombustible surface such as a concrete paver, gravel, or bare ground.

- All parts of the stove will get very hot while a fire is burning inside. Be sure not to touch any part of it with bare hands.

- Let the stove cool for at least 30 minutes after the fire has died out before handling.

Tips to Improve Engagement

- Most children have never used a can punch. Let them do it!

- There are few things in the world that will capture a child's sense of wonder like starting, building, and tending a campfire. This is a great opportunity to get them involved in the process.

- Gathering fire building materials will get the kids engaged in the activity. You'll want to gather three small piles of materials. The first will be fire tinder. This is the driest fluffy material you can find that will be ignited first. Dryer lint and cotton balls make perfect fire tinder. Dried grasses, pine needles, and very thin twigs (thinner than toothpicks) also make great fire lighting material for this pile. The second pile should be made of small dry sticks and twigs roughly the size of cotton swabs. This is the kindling that you'll place on the tinder as soon as it is ignited. The third pile will be made of dry sticks that range from pencil to thumb diameter size. This will be the material that ultimately fuels the stove.

- If you don't have a skillet or wok, this stove can also be flipped upside down and the bottom used as a cooking surface. Instead of cutting the fuel door toward the bottom of the can in the beginning, you will need to cut the door toward the top of the can as shown. The bottom will be a cooking surface with a fire inside. If you're cooking directly on the can, be sure to let the fire burn away any invisible coatings or linings that may exist on the can. A nice hot fire will do this in just a few minutes. Or simply cover the cooking surface with tinfoil.

Cook Bacon and Eggs in a Paper Bag

Age: 6+

MATERIALS NEEDED

- Brown paper bag
- 3–5 strips bacon
- 1–2 large eggs
- Campfire
- Cooking grate (optional)
- Long, sturdy stick (optional)

There's nothing quite like eggs and bacon for breakfast around camp—or in the backyard. The smell of bacon will rouse even the most tired camper from their tent. This project is just as much a science experiment as it is a lesson in campfire cooking.

No one believes that cooking eggs and bacon in a paper bag over the fire is possible until they see it for themselves. If you and your family take turns doing dishes, this is the perfect breakfast to volunteer your dishwashing services. The greatest feature about this old Boy Scout cooking trick is that the paper bag also serves as the plate when the cooking is done so there's no cleanup. You can either burn or compost the greasy leftovers. Cleaning pots and pans at camp is the worst!

It's true, a paper bag soaked in bacon grease does make the perfect fire starter. However, if you keep it away from open flames, it will not catch fire. It may char and smoke, but it will not ignite. Even though the paper bag with bacon and eggs inside are placed very close to red-hot coals, the wetness from the grease soaked into the paper prevents the paper from reaching an ignition point. The same principle applies to the process of boiling water in a plastic bottle. Yes, that's possible too.

The only thing better than no cleanup is the smell of this breakfast cooking. Between the smoky fire and sizzling bacon, this meal is destined to become a new family tradition!

INSTRUCTIONS

Step 1: Begin by placing strips of bacon in the bottom of the bag.

Step 2: Next, crack eggs right on top of the bacon.

Step 3: Make sure the wood in your campfire has burned down to coals. Fold over the top of the bag to keep the heat inside and place the bag directly over the hot coals of a fire. Do not let flames touch the bag or it will catch on fire. You can use a cooking grate or even spear the top of the bag with a stick and hold it over the fire like a marshmallow.

Step 4: Cooking times differ depending on the circumstances, but a good average is 15 minutes. After about 10 minutes, simply unfold the top of the bag and peek inside. Cook longer if necessary. When the eggs are cooked, the bacon is also done. When the cooking is done, just let cool for 10 minutes, tear off the top of the bag, and serve!

PARENT'S GUIDE

Safety Notes

- Hot bacon grease can cause some nasty burns. The keys to remember with this project are to not let the bag touch open flames while cooking and to let the bag cool after cooking before serving. The top of the bag is normally cool enough to handle at all stages throughout the cooking process.

Tips to Improve Engagement

- While placing the prepped bacon and egg bags on a cooking grate over the fire is easiest, there is something special about letting your child use a stick to hold the bag over the fire and cook for themselves. Yes, you run a risk of the bag catching on fire. But the risk is low as long as the fire has burned down to hot coals and there are no open flames. The stick can also be propped up to hang at a fixed height over the fire as well if a cooking grate is not available.

- Letting your kids prep their own bags is a critical part of the process. Consider having a few other ingredients on the table such as chopped peppers and onions. Cheese is also a great topping. Sprinkle it on after the cooking is done or it will burn.

- Burn your plate! Permission to *burn your plate* is always an unexpected surprise for the kids. And then they get to see what a great fire starter paper and bacon grease really makes.

Bake Orange Peel Ash Muffins

Age: 6+

MATERIALS NEEDED

- 4 oranges
- Knife
- Spoon
- 1 (8-count) package uncooked refrigerated cinnamon buns
- 8 large squares of tinfoil
- Tongs
- Fork

Fresh-baked gooey cinnamon buns are best enjoyed around a campfire with friends and family. Here's a camp cooking recipe that doesn't require an oven, fancy utensils, or messy cleanup. Whether you're in the backyard or on the trail, this project is two treats in one!

There are countless recipes for cooking over the campfire using tinfoil, but this is one of the easiest. In the span of 15 minutes you can enjoy a fresh orange and feast on your favorite brand of hot cinnamon buns prepared in mini baking pans upcycled from the leftover orange peels. Not only do the orange peels serve as the perfect-sized baking tray for cinnamon buns—they keep the buns moist and impart a delicious citrus flavor to the bread.

Campfire baking typically takes years of trial and error to get it right, but this awesome dessert is virtually foolproof. One of the best tips I can give you for cooking over any campfire is to let the wood burn down to a bed of coals that provides a hot, steady temperature. Cooking in a raging campfire is nearly impossible unless you want charred marshmallows. So start your fire and pile on some wood at least 30–45 minutes before you're ready for this treat. By that time, the coal bed should be just right.

INSTRUCTIONS

Step 1: Cut the oranges in half. One orange will make two mini cinnamon bun baking pans.

Step 2: Use the spoon to carefully scoop out the orange. It's okay to leave some of the orange inside the rind if it's stuck. This will help to impart an orange flavor to the cinnamon buns. Enjoy the fresh orange that has been scooped out!

Step 3: Open the cinnamon bun package and place one cinnamon bun into the cavity of each half orange peel cup.

Step 4: Place each peel with cinnamon bun onto a large square of tinfoil. Bring two opposite sides together and fold down the top a few times. Then flatten and fold in each end to completely enclose the orange peel and cinnamon bun. This not only protects the food from ash but also helps to keep the moisture inside for a steaming effect.

Step 5: Use the tongs to place the foil packages into the hot coal bed. Coals are created when the wood from a campfire burns down and breaks apart. The heat from hot coals is much steadier than from flames. Cooking times differ depending on the circumstances, but a good average is 15 minutes. After about 10 minutes, use the tongs to take out one of the packages. Let it cool for a couple minutes and check doneness by pulling up the centermost part of the roll with a fork to check that it still doesn't look raw. Cook longer if necessary.

PARENT'S GUIDE

Safety Notes

- The biggest concern here is when kids let the excitement of eating fresh-baked cinnamon buns overrule necessary waiting times for cooling off. Always place the tinfoil packages in the campfire and remove them from the campfire using tongs, and wait at least 5 minutes before attempting to open them.

Tips to Improve Engagement

- What else can you think of to bake inside of an orange peel? Biscuits and s'mores are two other fun options!

- Definitely let your kids do the dirty work of scooping out the orange and preparing the half-peel containers. This is all part of the fun.

- The doneness of many baked goods can be checked by inserting a toothpick to see if it comes out clean, meaning it's done. If there is residue on the toothpick, it's not yet finished. This is a great cooking lesson in general for kids of all ages. If checking doneness, let them stick in a toothpick and try to determine whether it's ready or not.

- When prepping this project, don't miss the opportunity to get your kids involved in building the campfire. Building a fire properly and safely is a lifelong skillset that should start early. Every opportunity to learn about campfire building and safety is a good one! Consider having roasted hot dogs or corn on the cob that can be cooked over the open flames while the fire is burning down to hot coals.

Bake Stick Bread

Age: 4+

Stick bread, also called twist bread, is a fun and whimsical campfire treat that hearkens back to simpler times. Baking bread around a campfire has a deep history in cultures all over the world. From Native American fry bread to Scotland's bannock, bread was a staple food almost everywhere.

MATERIALS NEEDED

- Campfire
- Cooking stick (as described in Step 1)
- Pocketknife
- 1 (8-count) package crescent rolls
- Butter and honey (optional)

To make twist bread, you must first let a hot fire burn down to coals. Hardwoods like oak and hickory are best for baking coals. The steady heat from hot coals is imperative when baking any kind of bread. Don't attempt this over the finicky and flickering flames of a campfire. You'll just end up with unevenly cooked and partially burnt bread.

As the name suggests, stick bread is baked on a stick. The dough is twisted around a stick that is roughly between the diameter of a thumb and a hot dog. If the stick is too thin it will bend and break. Conversely, if it's too thick, it's too heavy for kids to hold. A good time to gather baking sticks is while the fire is burning down to coals. Good stick options are those cut from hazel, basswood, willow, birch, or maple. Steer clear of resinous woods such as pine and spruce. Not only are they highly combustible, but they can also impart a bitter flavor to your bread.

I prefer to cut a fresh green stick, though it isn't necessary. ("Green" refers to a branch cut directly from a living tree.) When cutting fresh green branches for stick bread, hot dogs, or marshmallows over the fire, be selective in your harvest. Unlike popular belief, selectively pruning a tree or sapling of branches doesn't have to be destructive to the wilderness. In fact, if you do it right, it can help the tree thrive, and you can be a steward of the wilderness. For example, if two small saplings are growing close together, cutting one will give the other a chance to grow, rather than both suffering in competition. Or trimming a deformed branch from a tree can allow other healthy branches to grow. Regardless, the hunt for the perfect stick is all part of the fun.

INSTRUCTIONS

Step 1: Let your campfire burn down to hot coals. Baking with the steady heat from a hot coal bed is important to the success of this project. Use a pocketknife to carve and peel away the bark along the last 12 inches of any green stick you collect. This gives a nice clean surface to wrap your bread around. If using a seasoned (not freshly cut) stick or one purchased from a store, be sure to clean it before use.

Step 2: Open the crescent roll package and roll the dough into 12- to 18-inch sections that are about the thickness of your thumb.

Step 3: Wrap these rolled lengths of bread evenly around the peeled or cleaned end of your stick.

Step 4: One method of cooking is to hold the sticks with your hand like roasting a marshmallow. Or you can prop your stick beside the fire any number of ways to passively bake while you prepare the butter and honey! Either way, be sure to evenly bake the bread by regularly rotating the stick every 2–3 minutes. Cook until golden brown and there's no gooey dough on the inside. Most stick bread is finished in about 15 minutes, but times can vary greatly depending on the conditions and fire used.

PARENT'S GUIDE

Safety Notes

- The same rules apply to this project as when roasting marshmallows. Use common sense around the fire and let the bread cool for a few minutes after baking, and everything should turn out just fine.

Tips to Improve Engagement

- You don't have to use pre-packaged rolls! If you want to really get your hands messy, pull out your favorite bread recipe and let your kids help make the dough from scratch. Few children get the opportunity to bake from scratch these days, and it will be a great learning opportunity to see the project arch—from ingredients to finished stick bread.

- Take stick bread to the next level by choosing a stick that is the same diameter as a hot dog. Then, after the stick bread is finished baking, carefully slide the fully baked spiral bread from the stick and insert a roasted hot dog inside. Top with ketchup and mustard and you've made your own campfire pig in a blanket.

- Consider using packaged cinnamon bun or raisin bread dough instead of plain bread. If it's doughy and you can roll it into strands, then you can likely make stick bread from it!

Project 19

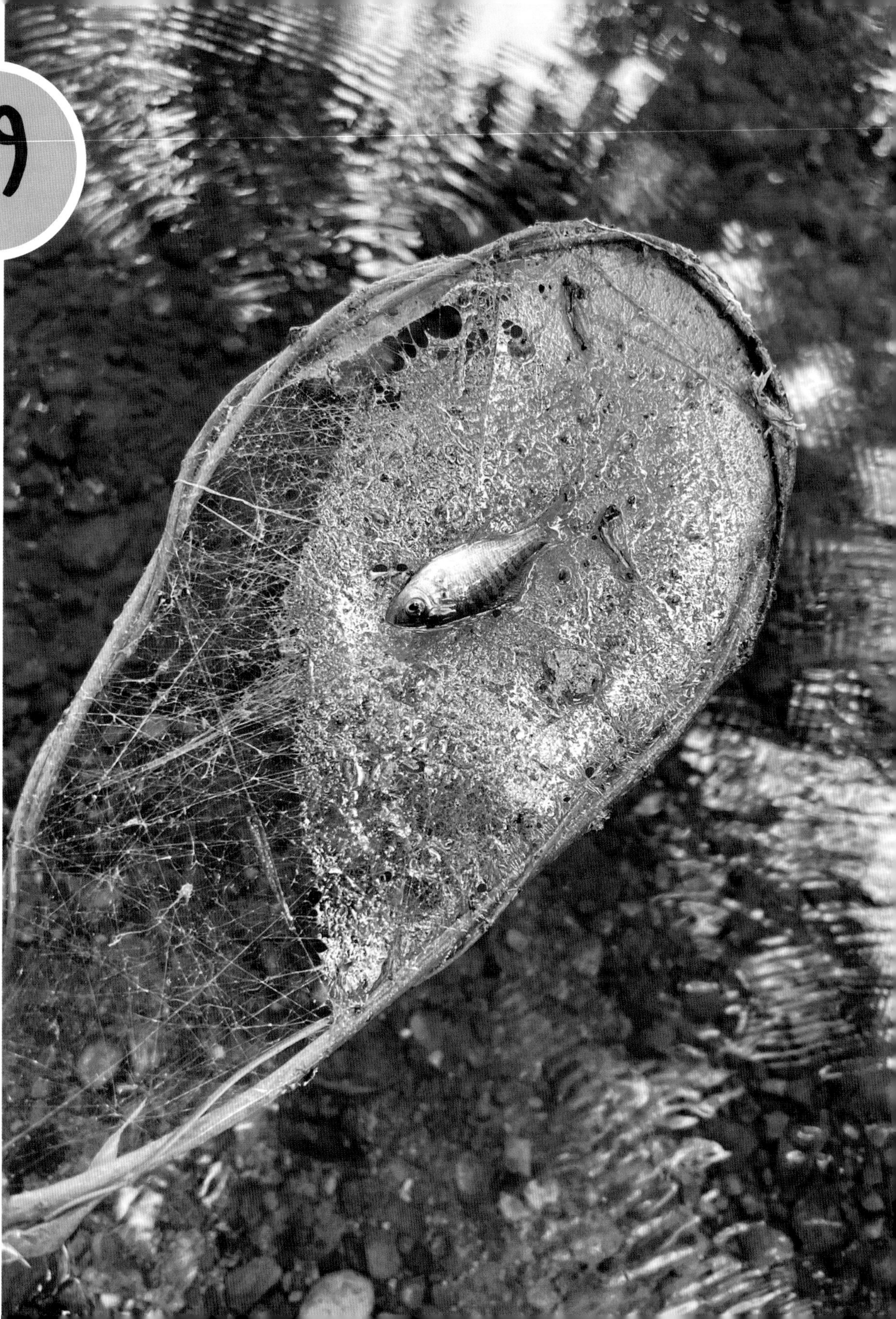

Catch Minnows (and Other Fishing Bait) with Spiderwebs

Age: 3+

MATERIALS NEEDED

- Flexible Y-forked branch
- Spiderwebs

Weaving a net for catching minnows or other fishing bait in the wild is no simple task. It requires a hefty supply of nice-quality twine, ample time, and previous weaving experience. But a nearly ready-made net already exists in nature if you just think outside of the box. Spiders are master net weavers—far more experienced than we could ever hope to be. And the webs they weave are made from one of the most amazing materials on earth—spider silk!

Did you know spider silk is five times stronger than steel of the same diameter? That's some incredible strength. Scientists have been trying for decades to replicate the strength and stretchiness of spider silk, but it seems to be a material that just can't be made in a lab. It is unique to our eight-legged little friends.

The webs you'll need for this project are the big ones that stretch between trees and under porches that act as nets for catching bugs. You will create your own net by sweeping a frame made from a branch through several spiderwebs. As they stick to the frame and layer on top of one another, you will be able to build a surprisingly strong net for catching minnows and more!

Not only is this project a great opportunity for kids to learn about spiders and spiderwebs but it also teaches one of life's most important skills—resourcefulness. The idea of using spiderwebs to make a bait net will come as a surprise at first, but as they see it come together, it will make more sense.

INSTRUCTIONS

Step 1: When it comes to spiderweb bait nets, a small frame hoop of less than 6 inches in diameter is ideal. A frame hoop can easily be made from a flexible Y-forked branch as shown here. Mulberry, willow, birch, and elm are all wonderful choices for net frames like this. The wood must be green and flexible. Brittle or dry branches will not work. The branch should be cleaned of its leaves and any other sharp pieces before proceeding. Leave the Y-forks long so they can be wrapped around each other to form a hoop.

Step 2: Form a hoop from the Y-forks that is 6 inches in diameter or less. The hoop frame is held together under the tension of the wrapped forks. Unwieldy frames can be secured and tied using freshly peeled slivers of green bark, small pieces of twine, or tape.

Step 3: Once the frame is finished, you are ready to "sweep the net." This is the phrase I use for scooping up spiderwebs. The process is simple, but there is a slight nuance that warrants mention. Just as you sweep the net frame through a spiderweb, slightly spin the frame forward by rotating the handle between your fingers. This slight spin causes the web fibers to wrap and lock around the frame. Sometimes, bits of broken web will even attach to the web on the other side, which is a bonus. Large spiderwebs can be swept through the upper portion of the web and then the net frame can be spun forward and swept back through the bottom portion of the same web. This makes for a particularly good bond of web fibers. As you sweep webs, alternate each side of the net frame so that webs are applied to each side.

Step 4: The number of webs needed to form a sufficient bait net depends on the type of web and the type of bait desired. Sweeping just a few webs will catch

most flying or jumping insects. To catch a minnow and withstand the sweeping movement through water you may need upward of twenty webs. The good news is that net repairs are quite easy—simply find your nearest spiderweb to patch a hole or tear.

4a

4b

Here is a net made from about fifteen spiderwebs.

PARENT'S GUIDE

Tips to Improve Engagement

- Spiderweb nets aren't as durable as store-bought woven nets, so being a bit more careful when using them is a good idea. Thrashing a spiderweb net through sticks or brush will tear it apart pretty quick. When using in water, go a bit slower than you normally would with a store-bought net and it will hold up longer.

- There are no venomous spiderwebs, only venomous spiders. Although the spiderwebs won't hurt you, take precaution to not get bit by a spider. The easy way to do this is to make sure the spider isn't on their web when you sweep it. Inspect the net after each sweep to make sure you don't have a spider!

- Insects are not the only thing that spiderwebs catch. The silky fibers also collect morning dew. A spider never has to leave its web, even for a drink. Because of this, it is easiest to find spiderwebs in the morning when the dew is heavy. Consider going on a spiderweb hunt through a local park or field in the morning before the dew evaporates. Fall is the best time to spot spiderwebs with condensation on them.

- Sweeping webs is a great opportunity to pause and study the spiders that built them. You'll normally find them right in the middle of the web or lying in wait at the corner to pounce on a trapped insect. Take a picture and search the Internet for spiders that live in your locale. Study what those spiders eat, what their habits are, and other characteristics. Before long, your little one will be able to identify every spider in your region.

- Whether wading through shallow creeks in search of minnows or running in a park after grasshoppers, I would highly encourage you to give your child an opportunity to use the net they have made. Making something like this and then successfully using it to catch something, if even a fly, builds incredible confidence in the minds of children.

CHAPTER 5

GEAR AND TOOLS

There was once a time when all the gear and tools someone used were handmade or sourced from the wild. With online retailers and big-box stores, our children rarely see a glimpse into this world of nature-based creativity, ingenuity, and craftsmanship.

In this chapter's projects, you'll learn how to work with nature to make some amazing things. And you'll be learning some very rewarding skills in the process. From upcycled minnow traps and stone tools to pine pitch glue and fire building, you're about to get a crash course in outdoor resourcefulness.

What's unique about this chapter is that your children will make things that can be used to do something else. There is something special about making something with your own hands that is then used to achieve a goal of some kind. It builds confidence and competence. For example, they'll be on the hunt for pine sap to make a natural adhesive that can be used in future crafting projects. Or they'll be fashioning an impromptu berry basket from a leaf to go berry picking. These aren't just projects for display; they are projects meant for a purpose. This alone will give your little ones a sense of purpose as well.

The projects in this chapter will also help to foster a deep respect for nature and things that are made by hand. This perspective can lead to a more genuine appreciation for all of the resources our planet provides. After all, every material possession we own or see was once mined, sourced, harvested, or derived from the earth.

Make Pine Pitch Glue

Age: 6+

Nodules on pine bark.

One of the most popular tools for crafting is a hot glue gun. Hot glue is a type of glue called a thermo-glue. This means you have to heat it up to use it. But what if I told you that Indigenous peoples were using a form of hot glue for thousands of years before anyone ever had the idea for a hot glue gun?

That's right: The original hot glue for affixing arrowheads and spearpoints onto wooden shafts for hunting was made by using all-natural materials that can be found and created in the wild. And this glue can be made today by you! You'll need a campfire (or candle) and two easy-to-find ingredients—pine sap and charcoal—plus just a few other simple items.

Pine sap oozes from a pine tree when it is injured. It is a sticky substance that seals the wound and helps to protect the tree from infection. When it oozes from the tree, pine sap hardens and forms crusty nodules. These pine sap nodules are easy to miss to the untrained passerby. But a wise traveler can pick them off (it doesn't hurt the tree) and use them for making pine pitch glue.

Although sticky, pine sap isn't strong enough to be used as glue by itself. It needs a hardening agent. For this you will use charcoal from a campfire. Charcoal is made up of the black pieces of charred wood left over after a campfire has burned out and cooled. It is not the white ash, but instead the carbonized pieces of wood that remain. Make sure the fire has cooled all the way before collecting these pieces of charcoal. These chunks of carbon can be crushed up into a powder and mixed with the pine sap to make a very strong thermo-glue, called pine pitch glue.

In the steps that follow you'll learn exactly how to make this Stone Age adhesive for yourself. The next time you run out of hot glue for crafting, forgo the trip to the store and head to the nearest pine grove instead!

INSTRUCTIONS

Step 1: First is the ratio for mixing. We want to mix roughly 3 parts pine sap to 1 part charcoal. This doesn't have to be perfectly exact, but too much charcoal will make very brittle glue. Just estimate the amounts and move forward.

Step 2: Grind the chunks of charcoal into powder. You can easily do this with a small rock. You can do this inside of the metal tin or on a flat solid surface. It's a messy job, but it is very important to grind the charcoal into as fine of a powder as you can. The finer the powder, the higher the quality of glue.

Step 3: Place the pine sap nodules into the tin and slowly heat the bottom using a candle. You can also use a grill or place the metal tin next to a campfire. You need just enough heat to melt the sap nodules. It won't take long. You can hold the tin over the flame of a candle with the pliers or rest it across two rocks as shown here.

Step 4: As the pine sap melts, stir it with the powdered charcoal using a small stick. Be careful; melting pine sap is very hot and can burn you. The goal is to have a nice smooth consistency when everything is thoroughly mixed together. If it is really chunky, you may need to add more pine sap to provide more liquid.

Step 5: Once everything is mixed well, you can simply remove your tin from the heat using the pliers and let the glue cool until you need to use it. But I recommend making what's called a "pitch stick." As the glue cools, you can use your stirring stick to collect the goopy glue while it is still warm and pliable. It will eventually cool off enough to shape on the end of the stick with your fingers. This ball of glue is now ready for storage. The good news is that you can keep it anywhere that isn't hot. When you need to use it, simply roll the end of the pitch stick over a flame to heat and soften the glue—just like hot glue. When it is nice and soft, dab it on like a glue stick and use it on your project before it cools!

PARENT'S GUIDE

Safety Notes

- Only make pine pitch glue on a noncombustible surface away from anything flammable.

- Whenever melting anything, be very careful! Melting pine sap can cause burns, so always handle the small metal container with a pair of pliers.

- Pine sap is not only a perfect glue ingredient but also a perfect fire starter. It is extremely flammable. Because of this, you don't want to expose it to direct fire flames. It *will* catch on fire. This is true while melting and mixing the glue as well as reheating it to use it for crafting. If the pine sap or glue catches on fire, move it away from the flame using pliers and blow it out like a birthday candle.

Tips to Improve Engagement

- Collecting pine sap is great fun. My own children take great pride in being able to spot a big fat pine sap nodule. It's like finding a hidden treasure that no one knows about. Don't miss the opportunity to take your kids on a pine sap hunt. A flathead screwdriver is the perfect tool for prying them from the tree, and you can keep the kids entertained for hours doing this at a local park or pine grove.

- A fun project to immediately use your pine pitch glue on is to make Popsicle stick ninja throwing stars. Simply use your pine pitch glue to glue the center of a few sticks together and throw them for accuracy in the backyard.

Make a Plastic Water Bottle Fish Trap

Age: 4+

Unfortunately, plastic water bottles can be found in and along almost every body of water in the world. Not only is this project a great way to talk about the importance of upcycling and reusing plastic water bottles—it also teaches a potentially lifesaving skill if your child is ever lost in the wilderness.

- Used clear plastic water bottle
- Scissors
- Handful of small rocks
- 1 cracker or ¼ piece of a slice of bread
- Duct tape
- 24-inch piece string

For centuries, funnel-shaped traps have been placed in waterways to catch fish for bait and sustenance. The classic fish trap has a funnel-like entrance with a small hole that leads into an enclosed area. Bait is placed inside the trap to encourage the fish to enter. Once inside, the fish aren't cunning enough to find their way back out through the little entrance hole.

With this knowledge, you can quickly and easily turn a used plastic bottle into a mini fish trap that can catch small minnows living in the waterways near your home. This trap functions in the same exact way as funnel traps used by various cultures all over the world. The great news is that it can be made in under 5 minutes.

Almost any plastic bottle size will work. I've seen these made from small 12-ounce bottles as well as 1-gallon containers. However, to see the minnows inside, you should use a clear plastic bottle. Stay away from cloudy or colored plastics if possible.

This skill hearkens back to a day and time when food was harder to come by. In the world today it's easy for us to forget that food wasn't always so readily available. Understanding this is important. There is no better way to illustrate this than to spend time making a trap and then waiting potentially hours for it to successfully catch something. Building the trap teaches hand-eye coordination, resourcefulness, and ingenuity. Waiting on its success teaches patience.

INSTRUCTIONS

Step 1: The first step is to cut off the top (mouth) of the water bottle that will form the inverted funnel. Use the scissors to cut about 1–2 inches below where the taper of the mouth stops.

Step 2: Cut a series of small holes or slits around the middle of the bottle. These will allow the bottle to fill with water and sink to the bottom when the trap is set. Do not make the holes so big that little minnows can get out. They can be any shape or size, just keep them small.

Step 3: Place the rocks into the bottom of the bottle. These will weigh the bottle down under the water so that it doesn't float. Then, tear up the equivalent of one cracker or a quarter piece of bread and place it inside the bottle also. This will be the bait that will entice the minnows inside.

Step 4: Invert the top piece that you cut off as shown like a funnel into the body of the bottle. This inverted funnel is where the minnows will enter the trap in search of the bait. They won't be able to find their way out. With some bottles, this piece will pressure fit snugly all on its own. If it is loose, you'll need to secure it in place. A couple pieces of duct tape work well for short-term use.

Step 5: Finally, poke a hole through the edge of the top near the funnel and tie on a long piece of string that will be used to anchor the bottle to the shore. Sink the bottle at the edge of water where you've spotted minnows before and tie off the other end of the string to a nearby stake, tree, rock, or stick. The trap will perform best when it is laying on its side on the bottom in a shallow area where minnows frequent. Now the trap is set. Leave and come back in a couple hours to check it!

PARENT'S GUIDE

Did You Know?

- Humans use about twelve million plastic bottles per minute and Americans themselves purchase about fifty billion water bottles a year! (That's thirteen bottles per month per person!) If we could avoid buying these bottles and instead use reusable bottles, we could save almost 156 bottles each year. And that's good news because virtually every piece of plastic that has ever been made still exists in some shape or form!

Tips to Improve Engagement

- What did you catch? Even catching a minnow can be a learning experience. This is a great opportunity to learn about what types of fish live in the waters near where you live. When you catch a minnow, search the Internet for "minnows that live in" and then type the body of water or place where you live. Help your kids to find out what species of fish they've caught and then learn about how big it gets, whether it's native or invasive, what it eats, and more. These are fantastic and unique opportunities to study and learn about local wildlife up close and personal.

- It's never too early to talk to kids about trying to reduce the use of single-use plastic items such as water bottles. Plastic bottles can take up to 450 years to degrade, so any that end up in the outdoors are going to be there for a very long time!

Make a Tulip Poplar Leaf Berry Basket

Age: 3+

Before plastic buckets, glass bottles, and woven fabric tote bags, people made containers from all-natural items such as plant fibers, tree bark, clay, and wood. Oftentimes these containers were very time- and labor-intensive to make and were consequently passed on from generation to generation.

However, all naturally made containers don't have to be complicated or require a great deal of time to manufacture. One such container that can be assembled in just a few minutes is made from the leaf of the tulip poplar tree (*liriodendron tulipifera*).

The tulip poplar tree is native to the eastern half of the United States, where it grows to be one of the largest trees in the forest. It gets the name from its tulip-shaped bloom, which has six yellow petals with orange splotches at the bottom. The seeds form inside of winged samaras that helicopter in the wind for long distances in later summer.

The leaf of the tulip poplar tree is very unique, resembling the outline of a cat's head. In fact, using it as such is a project I detail in the Parent's Guide section that follows. Tulip poplars grow tall, straight, and largely without branches until the top. For this reason, tulip poplar was once a very popular tree choice for building log cabins.

But one cool trick that few people know is how to quickly fashion a 1–2 cup berry harvesting basket from the green tulip poplar leaf. It's as if Mother Nature knew you might one day need an impromptu harvest basket while hiking during berry season!

INSTRUCTIONS

Step 1: You'll need to find the leftover spike that holds the winged tulip poplar seeds in the center of the tulip-shaped bloom. These are typically scattered everywhere underneath the tree from the previous year. You can't miss them. Look for fallen branches and you'll likely still find them attached to the tips. They look like a perfectly shaped awl, and you will use it as such!

Step 2: Choose the largest green tulip poplar leaf you can find and turn it upside down with the stem (petiole) pointing upward on a solid surface. Tip: Look for young tulip poplar trees; they have larger leaves!

Step 3: Now fold up the bottom portion (the actual top) of the leaf as shown and hold it down with your finger or a small weight.

Step 4: Fold the right side in toward the middle.

Step 5: Finally, fold in the left side of the leaf and use the awl-shaped spike receptacle to pierce through all three parts (bottom leaf lobe, right leaf lobe, and left leaf lobe) and hold everything together. The leaf stem can serve as a handle and can even be tied through a shirt buttonhole for hands-free picking. A large tulip poplar leaf basket will hold 1–2 cups of berries!

PARENT'S GUIDE

Tips to Improve Engagement:

- This is a great opportunity to knock out two projects at once. Bring along your leaf rubbing journal and record the tulip poplar leaf before fashioning it into a berry basket.

- A fun bonus art project is to use tulip poplar leaves as painting canvases for cat faces. Leaves at all stages can be used or even pressed in books for future use. I've included a photo to help get your cat-painting creative juices flowing.

- The tulip poplar is the state tree for Indiana, Kentucky, and Tennessee. What is your state tree? Look up the history of your own state tree and go find one!

- If you live in an area devoid of tulip poplar trees, search for a sycamore leaf. These are similarly shaped and will work as a close second. You'll have to improvise the spike by carving your own!

Carve a Paint Stick Hand Reel

Age: 6+

By 1943, a survival fishing kit was standard equipment on all lifeboats and life rafts used by the US Navy, US Coast Guard, Naval Air Forces, and Army Air Forces. This fishing kit is now known as the World War II Emergency Fishing Kit. It was a rolled canvas organizer with several items, including a large hook for snagging, a harpoon, a folded dip net, several hooks, and a few wooden hand reels.

- Paint stirring stick
- Printed template (optional)
- Scissors
- Pencil
- Pocketknife or small scroll saw
- Markers or paints
- About 25 feet fishing line
- Small fishing hook
- Fishing bobber

A hand reel is a tool for fishing that doesn't use a pole or modern mechanical reel. It is a method of fishing that dates back thousands of years. It is very simple and fun once you get the hang of it. At its core, a hand reel is a simple spool of fishing line with a hook on the end of it. The fishing line is manually uncoiled, and the lure is cast into the water by hand. Then it is wound back on the spool as the bait is brought back to shore. Another term for this type of fishing is *handlining*.

Handlining is a minimalist type of fishing. Because of that, hand reels are very compact and well suited for small survival kits. Although different types of hand reels are marketed and sold all over the world, you can easily make your own at home with materials you likely already have around the house.

There are many benefits to making your own hand reel. Many handmade crafts when finished are simply put up on a shelf or hung on a wall for display. The hand reel is meant to be used! After this project is finished you will be able to use your new hand reel to catch fish for sport or food. Now that's an outdoor craft that keeps on giving!

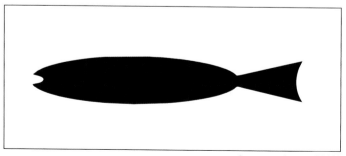

Copy template at 200%

INSTRUCTIONS

Step 1: The first step is to pick up a free paint stick at the hardware store. This will be the reel portion of your hand reel. Although you can make your hand reel any shape you wish, I recommend printing out my free template at the online resource page I've created for this book: CreekStewart.com/FamilyGuide. Cut out the fish shape with scissors and trace it with a pencil onto the paint stick.

Step 2: Use your pocketknife or small scroll saw to carefully carve out the traced wooden template. Paint sticks are very prone to splitting, so try your best to make small careful cuts.

Step 3: The best part of making your own wooden hand reel is decorating it. Take as long as you need to personalize your hand reel to make it uniquely yours. Use colored markers, paint, or any other kind of decorating tools you can think of to make your hand reel one of a kind! Note: Anything that washes away with just water might not be a good idea. This is, after all, for fishing!

Step 4: Tie one end of the fishing line around the tail as shown. This anchors your line onto the hand reel so that it doesn't come off the spool while using it.

Step 5: Finally, wrap roughly 25 feet of fishing line longways on the hand reel. If you're using my template, there is a V on the tail and notch for the mouth that holds the line in place. Finish by tying on a small fishing hook and attaching a bobber. Now you're ready to go hunt for worms and go fishing!

PARENT'S GUIDE

Safety Notes

- Paint sticks are very prone to splitting while carving. You will want to help your child carve if they are not familiar with using a knife. Please see my knife handling tips in the project titled "Carve an Old Man Face in a Bar of Soap" in Chapter 3. An alternative to carving is to use a small manual scroll saw.

Tips to Improve Engagement

- Don't underestimate the decorating stage of making this hand reel. My kids have just as much fun coloring their hand reels as they do using them for fishing! Encourage them to be creative. Our hunter-gatherer ancestors were known to lavishly and meticulously decorate their tools and hunting implements. It was a sign of individuality and pride of ownership. This is an important and fun part of the process. Don't skip it.

- Obviously, the best part of making a hand fishing reel is the moment your kids get to use it. This type of fishing reel is best used with red worms while fishing for bluegills and sunfish at the edges of ponds and streams. Make a big deal out of not only making the hand reel but using it. My son insisted that we cook and eat the first fish he caught on his hand reel, even though it was an undersized bluegill. He was so proud of that moment and made sure that everyone had a bite at the dinner table. His experience with the hand reel was far more than just making it, and I encourage yours to be too.

Abrade a Slate Arrowhead

Age: 4+

MATERIALS NEEDED

- Slate pieces (¼ inch thick, ideally flat on both sides)
- Flat, abrasive stone surface
- 16 ounces water

Before metal forging was mastered, many different types of rocks were fashioned into a variety of tools, including knives, axes, digging sticks, spearpoints, and arrowheads. Stone tools were once used by all peoples in all parts of the world. In fact, these stone artifacts are unearthed and found all the time.

Many types of rocks were used to make stone tools. Some rocks were shaped through knapping, the process of chipping away pieces of the stone to make the desired shape. Knapping was done using hammerstones, and even hard deer antlers. Flint and chert are two types of stone that were masterfully knapped into spearpoints and arrowheads.

Other rocks, such as granite, were shaped through abrading, the process of grinding a rock against another rock. This process slowly grinds away pieces of the rock until it reaches the desired shape. It can be a great way to make stone tools. One type of stone that was abraded to make knife blades and arrowheads was slate.

Slate is a very fine-grained sedimentary rock that can be made from clay, volcanic ash, and other minerals. It is created over time with pressure. It forms in layers and stands out from other rocks because it can be found in flat sections. Layers of slate can be found in creek beds and on the sides of roadways that have been cut through hills or mountains. It's also common for small pieces of slate to be found mixed in with landscaping stone. Just look for thin, flat gray rocks with angular edges, and it's likely a type of slate or shale (a close relative).

Abrading slate arrowheads is a perfect introduction into the incredible world of stone tools. Not only can it be easily accomplished by small children—it requires no experience or fancy tools. Helping your children to make their own stone tools is a perfect opportunity to teach how similar tools were used by our hunter-gatherer ancestors to survive in the wild.

INSTRUCTIONS

Step 1: Find a piece of slate. Rock landscaping beds are a great place to look. If the landscaping area isn't on your own property or someone's you know, simply ask the owner if you can have a piece of slate from it. I've never had someone say no! Rocky lake and creek shores are a common spot for slate as well. It's important to start with a piece of slate that is close to the size of the arrowhead you want to make. This helps to reduce the amount of time it takes abrading. If necessary, use a hammerstone (just a fancy word for another rock) to carefully knock off pieces from the edge. Wear safety glasses if you do this. Cross your fingers and hope for the best. Only do this if your piece of slate is much larger than the size of the arrowhead you have in mind.

Step 2: Now you need to find a grinding stone. This can be any stone surface that is flat and abrasive. The bottom of a brick or concrete paver works great. A flat sandstone will also work. Have some water handy because everything from here on out will be wet-ground.

Step 3: Pour water on the grinding stone and start grinding an edge of the slate to a pointed triangle shape (acute isosceles triangle). Just imagine the shape of an arrowhead. Press down firmly and abrade the slate quickly against the grinding stone. You'll quickly see the water change to a dark color as bits of slate grind away and create a muddy slurry.

Step 4: This is the shape after several minutes of grinding, applying water occasionally and liberally. Notice how both sides are ground flat to create a pointed tip. Next is to shape and flatten the back of the arrowhead. Arrowheads can take many forms. Be creative. Yours doesn't have to look exactly like this one.

Step 5: Once you have a general triangle shape, it's time to abrade the notches. These are small indentations on the back sides of the point that serve as lashing points when affixed to an arrow. This is done by abrading each side of the arrowhead along a sharp corner of your sanding stone or brick.

Step 6: With the sides, back, and notches abraded, it's time to grind the bevel of the arrowhead. This is a tapered grind along each side edge to make them sharper. You'll do this by holding the arrowhead at a slightly flat angle while abrading along the edges. You will be amazed at how sharp you get the edge bevel on a slate arrowhead. Once these bevels are sharpened, the arrowhead is ready for display or use!

PARENT'S GUIDE

Safety Notes

- If a hammerstone is used to shape the slate or break a larger piece of slate into pieces, it is a good idea to wear safety glasses. Any type of stone breaking can cause tiny sharp shards of stone to fly in all directions. A piece of slate in the eye will put an end to this project very quickly.

- The process described is the exact same as used by Indigenous people to create arrowpoints for bow and arrows, spears, and harpoons. Slate points can be abraded to be extremely pointed with very sharp beveled edges that are capable of piercing skin, clothing, furniture, and more. If using the arrow point as jewelry, consider abrading the point and edges a little dull to avoid any accidents while wearing it.

Tips to Improve Engagement

- A quick and easy secondary project after a slate arrowhead is completed is to quickly put it on display as a pendant. This can be easily done by twisting a short piece of wire or cord around the notches to form a hanging loop. A leather lace is the perfect necklace.

- Arrowheads were just one of many different tools and objects made from slate. Consider expanding your newfound slate abrading knowledge to create a new and more complicated piece. A slate knife blade affixed into a wooden handle is a great advanced project to test your skills even more. If you'd like to do this, you can download a free full worksheet detailing the steps at CreekStewart.com/FamilyGuide.

Start a Campfire Using a Ferro Rod

Age: 7+

Various types of ferro rods.

The knowledge to build a campfire safely and effectively is important. Whether for fun, camp cooking or downright survival, the campfire will always have a special place in our lives. By the end of this project, you'll be the go-to campfire starter in your family each time the need arises!

There are hundreds of ways to start a campfire. One of them is virtually foolproof and uses a fairly modern campfire starting tool called a ferrocerium rod. The ferrocerium rod is known by many names—*ferro rod*, *metal match*, and *modern flint striker* are just a few. It is without a doubt one of the most useful, effective, and affordable tools ever created.

Ferro rods come in many shapes and sizes. Ferrocerium is a metal made from iron (ferro), cerium, and a few other metals. Cerium has a very low ignition point. Consequently, scraping a ferro rod with enough speed and force removes little pieces of the metal while simultaneously creating heat from friction. This heat ignites the tiny shavings and creates sparks in the form of micro pieces of burning metal that can be thousands of degrees in temperature. You can use these tiny sparks to ignite tinder and build a campfire.

A very important component to successfully using a ferro rod is the tinder used. Tinder is the fibrous material that catches on fire when the sparks from the ferro rod are created. The perfect tinder material is a simple cotton ball. It is dry and fibrous.

Learning how to use a ferro rod to start a campfire is a skill that will be used many times throughout a child's life. It is a skill that teaches responsibility and instills trust. But more importantly, this is one of the few life skills that can actually save your child's life if they were ever lost in the wilderness. Campfires can keep them warm, cook food, boil and purify water, and signal for rescue.

Note: If you do not already have a ferro rod, I have included links to my favorites at the online resource page for this book at CreekStewart.com/FamilyGuide.

INSTRUCTIONS

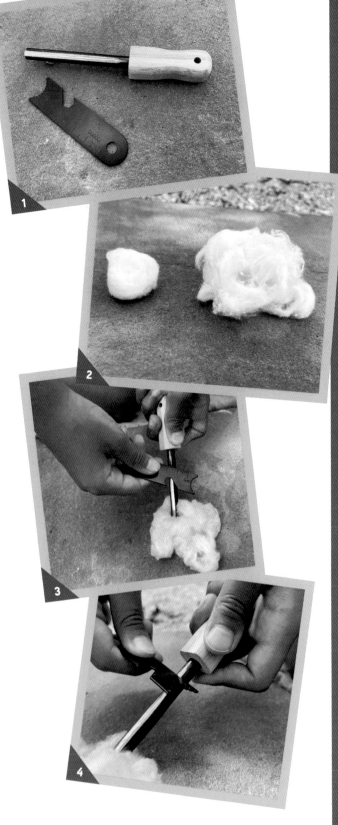

Step 1: All ferro rods have a thin protective coating. This helps to prevent corrosion. It must be scraped away to expose the metal underneath before you can make sparks. The ferro rod striker is almost as important as the ferro rod. The typical ferro rod comes with a small stamped metal striker. Some nicer ferro rods come with a more robust striker. Almost anything hard with a sharp edge will work as a striker, even a sharp rock. Use the striker that came with your ferro rod to scrape away the coating on the outside of the rod. Note: Before creating sparks, make sure your workspace is a solid noncombustible area that is free of anything flammable.

Step 2: Once you have your ferro rod coating scraped off a bit, it's time to prepare your tinder. All you need is one cotton ball for practice. You want to create as much surface area as possible in your tinder. Doing so increases the chances that the tiny sparks you'll be generating will ignite it. The best way to do this is to expose as many of the cotton fibers as possible. Pull apart and fluff up the cotton ball to create as much fiber surface area as possible. Once this is done, it is time to drive sparks into your tinder. This photo shows a regular cotton ball next to one that is prepared as tinder.

Step 3: An important note to make before striking is to "plant the tip of your ferro rod" in your tinder and against a hard surface such as a rock or dry, bare earth. This improves control and makes for a more solid strike. Fight the urge to "float" your ferro rod above your tinder and throw sparks through the air into it. The less distance your sparks must travel to reach your tinder, the better your chances of igniting it.

Step 4: Striking technique is imperative to generating large chunks of burning metal. When using a traditional stamped steel striker, the burr edge should be scraped down the ferro rod at a forward-facing angle of roughly

45 degrees as shown in the photo. It should be scraped with force, pressure, and purpose, not with weak, willy-nilly movements that lack gumption. I always tell my students to scrape like their life depends on it.

Step 5: Once you've determined your angle of attack and have the tip of your ferro rod firmly planted, it's time to strike and drive sparks into your fluffed-up cotton ball. Here is a practice strike to get sparks without the cotton ball.

Cotton ball ignited with ferro rod. Now it's time to add sticks and twigs to build the campfire.

PARENT'S GUIDE

Safety Notes

- Never use a ferro rod indoors. Only use it outside on a solid noncombustible surface such as a concrete/asphalt driveway, bare dirt, or concrete paver. The best spot to practice making a campfire is in a prepared campfire pit.

- Campfires should never be left unattended. A stray spark could blow away and create an unwanted fire.

- Always make sure campfires are extinguished with water until the coals are cool enough to touch.

Tips to Improve Engagement

- Of all the skills I teach in my in-person courses, responsible fire building is my favorite. Have a camera ready when your child ignites their first cotton ball. It is a moment you're going to want to capture. It will be excitement, awe, pride, accomplishment, wonder, and adventure all packed into one jaw-dropping stare. Trust me—it is going to be a framer. Revisit the photo and have them recount what they were thinking in the moments when the sparks landed, and the cotton set ablaze. Let them tell the story and speak greatness, confidence, and encouragement into their life.

- I've never met a child who doesn't love helping build a campfire, especially one where they have created the initial flame with their own two hands. Have materials on hand to take the flaming cotton ball to the next level and build an actual campfire. You'll need three piles of materials. First, you'll need two handfuls of dry grasses or something similar. When the cotton ball ignites, you'll put this on top. As the dry grasses ignite, add on two more handfuls of sticks and twigs that are about the diameter of toothpicks and cotton swabs. When these start to burn, place on two more handfuls of sticks and twigs that are roughly the size of No. 2 pencils. Work your way up from there.

CHAPTER 6

WILDERNESS SHELTERS

Shelter building is at the center of every imaginative childhood story. Whether it is a castle or a fort, there is something about the backyard shelter that sparks adventure in the minds of children. This is why every child wants a tree house or piles of pillows around the couch.

In this chapter you'll learn an assortment of shelter building skills that will help you and your children to quickly and safely build amazing structures in your backyard or wherever else your adventure leads you. From bedsheet tents to Arctic snow domes, your next night could be spent under the stars in a shelter your family built by hand. What a fantastic memory.

Although the shelters mentioned here are going to be really fun to build in the backyard, they aren't just for fun. These shelters are based on very practical and proven shelter building skills. When your child completes each of these projects, they will be equipped with a unique set of out-door skills that can take outside play to the next level. While perfect for backyard fun, these skills can also save their life if ever lost in the woods!

Shelter building is one of the most active outdoor activities there is. In some instances, it is downright hard work. But it is work that builds not only a cool structure but also character in your kids. The pride that comes from sheltering in a structure they built is truly priceless. Often-times the most rewarding results are those paid for with sweat equity.

26

Build a Debris Hut

- -

Age: 3+

Have you ever watched how a squirrel builds its nest in the trees? Or have you ever seen a mouse nest when you've turned over a log or rock? Both of these critters use grasses, leaves, sticks, twigs, mosses, and other forest debris to make a shelter that protects them from the rain, wind, snow, and cold. There is a lot to learn from these masters of survival!

A debris hut is the human version of what animals have been doing to stay warm and protected since the beginning of time. Without a campfire, your only heat source

is that which your body produces. A debris hut is specifically designed to capture and contain that body heat while at the same time being a barrier to the elements. It is not only an incredible survival shelter but an awesome one to build in the backyard for fun.

A key component to any good debris hut is insulative material, and lots of it. Natural insulation material includes leaves, grasses, mosses, bark, pine needles, and other similar forest debris. This debris serves two purposes. First, when packed in many layers, it is very effective at repelling rain and snow. Second, it creates dead-air space. Dead-air space between you and the elements is very important to staying warm. Leaves and grasses do a really good job at trapping pockets of dead-air space around a debris hut shelter. This dead-air space acts as an insulation barrier between you and the cold. This is the same way a big fluffy jacket keeps you warm.

Debris huts are built in two stages. First, a frame is erected using sticks. This frame creates a sleeping area inside and supports the insulation material that is piled on top. Second is the use of debris. Dry leaves (or similar) are piled on top of the stick framework to create the walls and roof of the shelter. Depending on the temperature, this wall of debris may need to be several feet thick to stay warm. However, if done correctly, you can stay warm with no fire or sleeping bag in a debris hut in freezing cold temperatures.

All children love to build forts! This project teaches basic shelter construction skills that will last a lifetime. It also instills a sense of respect and admiration for the forest critters who live in these types of shelters year-round. Finally, this is a valuable skill to know if ever lost in the wilderness. It can truly save your life.

INSTRUCTIONS

Step 1: The first step is to find three very important sticks. They should be sturdy, straight, and between 1–2 inches in diameter. They will need to support the weight of all the debris you'll be piling on top. Two of the sticks should be about 36 inches long with a fork at the top and the last stick should be one and a half times the length of the person who the shelter is built for.

Step 2: Create an A-frame structure by locking the forks of the two shorter sticks together at the top. The long pole will be a center roof ridge pole that will hold the A-frame front in place. The interior space of debris huts is very small for a reason. The less space you must warm with your body heat, the better. You should be able to get on your belly and slide backward through the A-frame door and be fully inside the shelter under the ridge pole.

Step 3: Now it's time to build the "dinosaur rib cage." Kids love that phrase. This is done by placing sticks at a 45-degree angle up against the roof ridgepole on both sides. They should match the height of the ridgepole and not extend beyond it. If they are too tall and stick out from the insulation, then rain will drip down the poles and into your shelter. These sticks don't have to be perfect, but they should not be rotten. The purpose of the dinosaur rib cage is to keep the insulation from falling into the shelter. Branches and sticks that have fallen on the ground from trees are the perfect sticks to be used for this.

Step 4: Here is what the structure should look like when the dinosaur rib cage is finished. Both sides should be clad with sticks at a 45-degree angle against the main central ridgepole.

Step 5: Now it is time to pile on forest debris. Pine needles are being used in this photo. Just like a roofer will lay shingles on a roof, you want to pile insulation from the bottom up. Doing so creates overlapping debris that helps to shield you from the rain if it comes.

Step 6: The thicker the debris wall, the more dead-air space you'll trap and the warmer and more protective the shelter will be. If you can see light from the inside, keep adding debris! Note: In a true "survival" debris hut, the floor and interior should also be packed with dry debris. If you live in an area devoid of forest debris, don't worry. I've taught this skill at local libraries for years and need to carry all my supplies with me. Great alternatives for forest debris are bales of hay or bales of pine needles that can be purchased from your local landscaping center. Do not try to use bales of straw. Straw is typically very short and does not work well for debris hut material.

PARENT'S GUIDE

Safety Tips

- Depending on the time of year, keep in mind that ticks could still be out and active. The key is a good-quality tick check after outside play and before bed at night. If you do find an embedded tick, I recommend sending it in for testing to see if it is infected with any of the common tick-borne illnesses.

- Whenever gathering leaves and forest debris for a shelter like this, it's important to be on the lookout for poison ivy and poison oak. This is also a great opportunity to teach your children how to identify both. If you or your children come in contact with either, the best way to reduce the effects is to immediately wash the exposed areas with soap and water and wash any clothing.

Tips to Improve Engagement

- This is a project that goes faster with lots of help, so consider inviting over friends to get involved.

- The key to getting into a debris hut is *low and slow*. Have your child get down on their hands and knees with their feet facing the door. Then they will slowly worm their way backward into the shelter. This is the best way to not disrupt and collapse the stick framework that holds it all together.

Make a Quinzee Snow Shelter

Age: 6+

MATERIALS NEEDED

- Snow
- Shovel
- Sticks (each about 18 inches long)

For centuries, people who lived in northern Arctic regions sheltered inside of igloos, huts made of snow and ice. It takes quite a bit of skill and very deep snow to make an igloo shelter. However, there is a snow shelter that's very similar in style but doesn't require the experience, skill, or deep snow. It's called a *quinzee*.

Building a quinzee snow shelter is the ultimate snow-day activity. In just a few hours, you can build and be sheltering inside of one of the coolest snow forts you've ever seen. And although building a quinzee in your backyard is just for fun, people have used them to stay alive in cold and snowy areas when no other shelter was available.

As long as you have enough snow to pile into a dome that is at least four feet tall in the middle, then you have the materials to build a quinzee. One principle that is important to understand when building a quinzee is a phenomenon called *sintering*, which is the fusing of snow particles. When you shovel snow into a pile and let that pile sit for several hours, all of the little snow crystals fuse together and create a large, connected mass of snow. This is the process that allows us to carve out the middle. Without the sintering effect, the snow would easily collapse under the weight of itself.

Even though inside of a quinzee is still very cold, snow is actually a good insulator. Your body heat, or the body heat of you and a few friends, can slightly increase the temperature inside. The real sheltering advantage is that the quinzee can protect you from the exposure to wind and more falling snow. You'll be surprised at how cozy it can be inside of a shelter made entirely from freezing snow!

INSTRUCTIONS

Step 1: Especially important in deep snow (1-plus feet), you'll need to stomp down or pack the area where you're building the quinzee. This can be done by walking the area in boots or snowshoes. The diameter of the base of the quinzee should be at minimum 1 and a half times the length of your body with outstretched hands. This gives head and foot room on the bed and takes into account the wall thickness at the base of the shelter. Note that it can be as large as you'd like, but if it's too small, you'll have space issues inside.

Step 2: This step is the second most labor-intensive part of the build. You'll need to shovel a pile of snow that's at least as tall as yourself and the diameter described in Step 1. This is where a shovel comes in handy. The shape should be as dome-like as you can make it, not too pyramid-shaped and not too flat-topped. Try to make it as dome-shaped as possible. After the snow is piled, it must be left to sinter. Depending on the conditions, this can take from one to several hours. Sintering is what allows you to carve out the inside and gives structure to the shelter's walls.

Step 3: To ensure the walls and roof of your dome-shaped snow shelter are thick enough to provide insulation and are also of uniform thickness all around, it is a good idea to insert depth gauge sticks all around the top and sides of the snow pile. These should be roughly 18 inches long and inserted to a depth of 12 inches into the mound roughly 12 inches apart from one another. When digging out the interior later, these sticks will serve as guides to alert you to stop digging when you see the ends. Notice the evenly spaced depth gauge sticks (willow) in this photo.

Step 4: Once the depth gauges are in place, it's time to begin the excavation process. The door opening should be small and not much larger than is required

to crawl inside. It should also be facing *away* from the wind. The door will be left at least partially open while sheltering inside and wind blowing directly into a quinzee can be devastating to its effectiveness. When hollowing out the interior, carve into the middle and go up toward the roof first. This eliminates the weight of the snow from above your head as fast as possible. This way, if the shelter does collapse, you've already eliminated excess weight. (See Safety Notes section.) Once you start to see the ends of your depth gauge sticks, begin carving more to the sides.

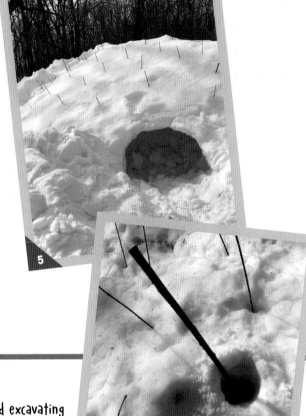

Step 5: With a little help, excavating the interior of a quinzee can be done in just a couple of hours.

PARENT'S GUIDE

Safety Notes

- There is a definite risk of collapse while building and excavating a quinzee. They are best built by two people just in case.

- Always sleep with a small shovel just in case!

- While excavating, dig up as fast as you can so that you can crouch as soon as possible. This way if there is a collapse, you're on your feet and can use the power of your legs to help get out.

- Never build a fire in a quinzee. Small candles are fine for light, but a fire will cause it to cave in.

- If sleeping in a quinzee, be sure to carve a small air hole about the diameter of your arm through the roof. This allows airflow in and out of the shelter (see photo).

Tips to Improve Engagement

- To drastically reduce the amount of time spent hollowing out a quinzee, snow can be piled on top of gear, backpacks, or even garbage bags stuffed with pillows. When you reach these items during the excavation process you can just pull them out and it saves having to dig out the entire interior!

- The best part of building a quinzee is crawling inside and enjoying the result of all your hard work. But if you want to make a memory that will last a lifetime, throw down some camping ground pads, grab your sleeping bags and spend the night.

Erect a Tarp Shelter

Age: 3+

MATERIALS NEEDED

- 5 feet strong twine or paracord
- Full bedsheet or larger
- Rocks
- 4 tent stakes

One of the quickest and easiest shelters to protect yourself from the rain, sun, wind, or snow is a tarp shelter. Tarp shelters of various designs date back to the beginning of humankind. Native Americans in North America used the hides of deer, elk, and buffalo to erect many different styles of tarp shelters, including the iconic cone-shaped tipi.

Tarps come in all different shapes and sizes. A tarp is essentially a sheet of material that you can configure as a shelter using rope, stakes, and anchor points. Your tarp doesn't have to be fancy or expensive. It can be anything from a sheet of plastic or a bedsheet to a painting drop cloth or old scrap piece of pool liner. Everyone has something that can be used for a tarp shelter.

Not only are tarp shelters just plain functional—they are also fun. Even though you'll learn only one shelter configuration in this project, you'll have the tools to configure the same tarp or bedsheet into many different shapes with a little creativity. From lean-tos and wedges to tunnels and A-frames, your creativity is the limit.

It is quite possible that shelter building is the one skill that evokes the most adventure in the imaginative minds of children. Depending on the child, the simple bedsheet tarp shelter outlined in this project will be a castle, camping tent, jail, cave, ice cream parlor, fort, survival shelter, safe zone, home base, kitchen, club headquarters, or one of hundreds of other imaginary structures that take place in the stories children make up when you encourage them to act on their creativity.

INSTRUCTIONS

Step 1: You'll need to find an anchor point such as a tree or fence post. The first step is to tie one end of a 36-inch piece of rope to your anchor point using a double half hitch knot as shown in the photo. To start, tie this approximately 48 inches from the ground, but you will adjust it a bit later.

Step 2: Now tie another double half hitch around the very middle of one of the long ends of the bedsheet. Place a small rock or marble under the fabric to create an improvised anchor point on the sheet. Tie your double half hitch around this rock. The peak of the tarp shelter is now tethered to your anchor point.

Step 3: Now you'll need to adjust the height of your string tied to the tree. Move this up or down the tree so that the front corner edges of the sheet just barely touch the ground.

Step 4: Stretch out and secure the back corners of the tarp. Create improvised grommets by tying a loop of rope using an overhand knot around each back corner of the bed sheet. Place a small rock on the underside of the bedsheet for an anchor point as before and tie around it.

Step 5: Pull the sheet back and drive a tent stake through each of these loops to pull the tarp taught.

Step 6: Tie the same improvised grommets on the front corners of the tarp and stake them to the ground as well. This completes your tarp shelter.

PARENT'S GUIDE

Bonus Learning

- If you find that this is a project your kids really like, then I want to give you a free downloadable copy of my pocket field guide titled *Survival Tarp Shelters*. In this guide I teach eight essential knots and nine different tarp configurations. These skills will expand your configuration options using a tarp. These are more advanced tarp shelter ideas and can fill an entire weekend of learning. Download this free PDF guide at the online resource page for this book at CreekStewart.com/FamilyGuide.

Tips to Improve Engagement

- How many different shelter configurations can you come up with using the knowledge you've learned? Challenge your kids to erect their own shelter style using some rope and the improvised grommet ideas listed earlier. Hint: larger sheets give more options.

- Consider planning an activity to play inside of the tarp shelter once it is finished. A card game or board game are always good options. Even better, let your child do their school homework in their new tarp shelter. The ultimate test is a backyard overnight with sleeping bags, s'mores, and ghost stories. I see a tarp shelter picnic in your future.

Make Mud and Straw Bricks

Age: 3+

Bricks are one of the oldest known building materials. Some of the first bricks ever used were formed from mud and dried in the sun. Later, clay and straw were used to make bricks. From Egyptian pyramids in the Middle East to the Pueblo People of Southwest America, clay and straw bricks have survived the elements for thousands of years. They are an incredibly durable building material and very simple to make, consisting of only mud (clay), water, and straw. Straw is optional but helps to prevent the bricks from cracking when there is a high clay content.

- Large container (optional for mixing)
- Small shovel
- Mud/clay
- 2 gallons water (to start)
- Straw
- Plastic containers

The ideal mud for brickmaking has at least some clay. However, any mud can be used to make bricks. The more clay in the mud, the longer the bricks will hold up to the elements. Clay-rich mud can be found along the eroded banks of a stream or pond or from a fresh construction site dig, such as when a foundation is excavated when building a home. If these areas aren't available to you, just use any dirt you have access to.

Traditionally, mixing the mud, straw, and water was done barefooted in a hole in the ground. A hole in the ground makes the perfect container for mixing if you don't mind making one in your yard. A larger container of some kind is a close second. Mixing barefooted as shown in the steps in this project is without question more fun for kids, but mixing in a 5-gallon bucket is an option as well. Either way, expect to get dirty! Other alternatives are large troughs and plastic kiddie pools.

Bales of straw from a local hardware store, pet supply store, or farmer are ideal, but if straw is not available, dried grass clippings will work as well. The straw works as a binding material to hold the mud together and prevent the bricks from cracking, especially when high in clay. The ratio I use of mud to straw is 3:1 by volume, but this can vary greatly (for example, one full 5-gallon bucket of mud mixed with one-third of a 5-gallon bucket of straw). Enough water should be added to wet all the mud and straw into a thick, goopy texture but not so much that it is runny and falls between your fingers. Freshly made bricks should hold up on their own.

Bricks for construction were originally formed using wooden molds so that each brick was the exact same size. For this project, however, I suggest using various plastic containers you can find around the house. From pie and bread tins to ice cube and cupcake trays, bricks of all shapes and sizes can be created. Once finished, the bricks can be used like building blocks to make miniature forts, castles, bridges, and blockades.

Giving kids the opportunity to make mud bricks is great fun. What child doesn't like playing with mud? Not only does this project encourage creativity and a hands-on tactile experience—children also get to learn basic construction principles that date back thousands of years. The idea that people once used mud and straw to build homes and structures is an amazing realization and will elicit many curious questions. And all bricks made using this process are environmentally friendly and 100 percent biodegradable!

INSTRUCTIONS

Step 1: The first step is to make your mud and straw mix. This can be done in a shallow hole in the ground or inside of a container like a 5-gallon bucket. If digging a hole, you can simply use the dirt dug from the hole to make the mud—just add water. If you can find soil with some clay content, that's best, but not imperative. Give your kids permission to get dirty during this phase! The mud mix should be wet and gooey but not so wet that it slips through your fingers. Add the straw to the mud and mix thoroughly in a ratio of roughly 3:1 (mud:straw). Remember, you can always add more water but you can't take it out!

Step 2: Once everything is mixed, it's time for pressing into molds.

Step 3: Start this step by wetting the inside of your mold containers. This helps the makeshift bricks to slip out easier for drying. Press the mud/straw mix into the molds and slick the top of each one smooth with a wet hand.

Step 4: Gently pop the bricks out of the molds onto the ground or a drop cloth for drying. If the sides of the bricks slump down, then this means your mix is too wet. You want your bricks to hold their shape when not in the mold.

Step 5: Drying the bricks in the sun is best. Smaller bricks made in ice trays will be dry in a couple hours, while it might take a full day for larger bricks to dry. Once the bricks are dry, they will last a very long time if they aren't crushed or left out in the rain. Mud bricks are still uncovered in archeological digs today that are thousands of years old!

PARENT'S GUIDE

Interesting Fact

- Mud bricks are making a comeback among those seeking environmentally friendly building materials. Not only are mud bricks inexpensive to make but they are also very comparable to modern red bricks and even concrete block when it comes to maintaining temperatures inside the home. In addition, mud bricks can be sourced locally and are easily disposed of if the structure should ever need to be demolished.

Tips to Improve Engagement

- Wet mud can be used as mortar between bricks to build walls for small structures. Consider making enough bricks to build a small house for local fairies or goblins that may frequent your backyard in the wee hours of the morning. Keep track with your kids at how long this structure lasts in the elements. Its life span may surprise you!

Project 30

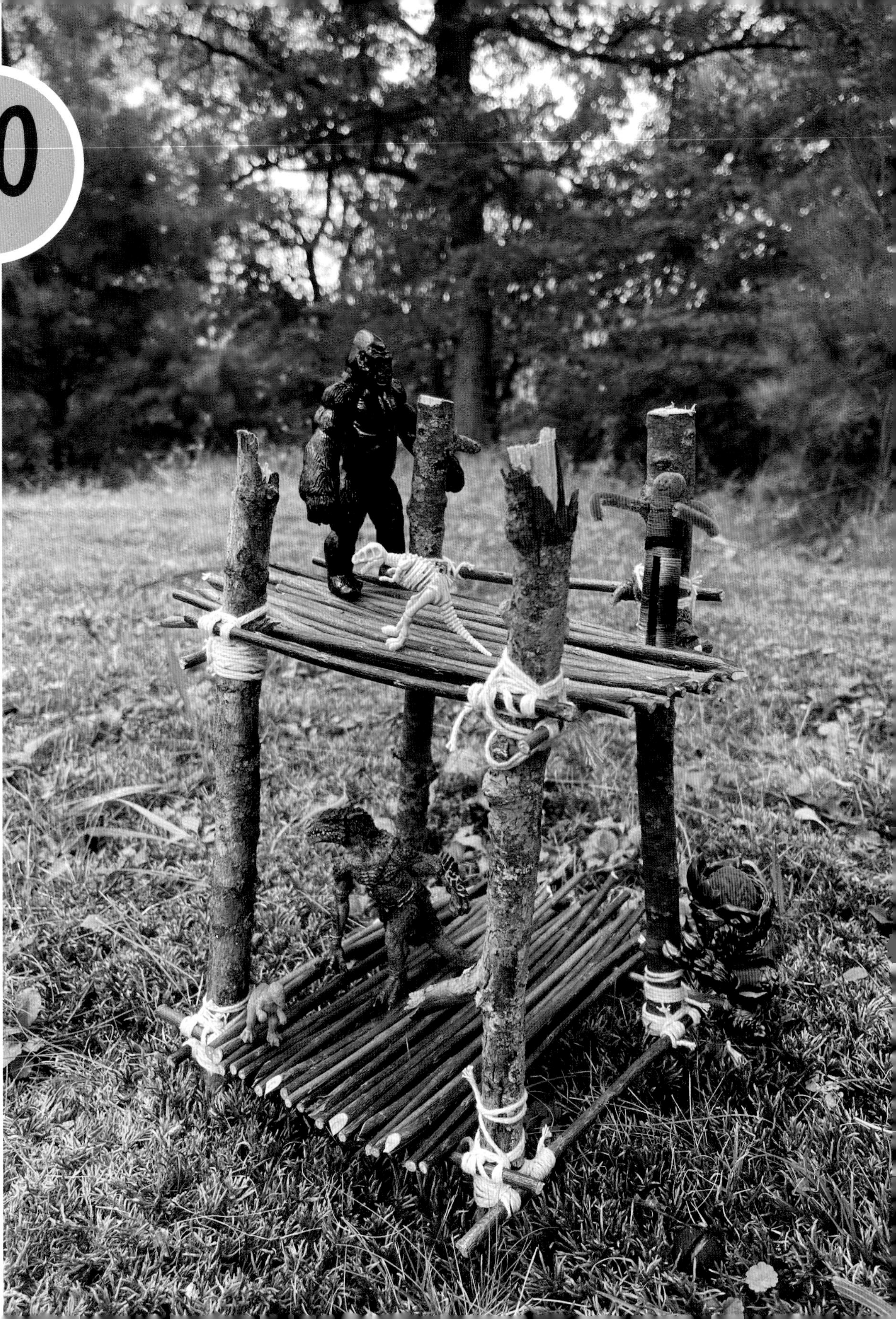

Lash a Tower

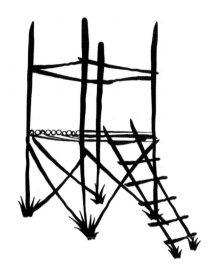

Age: 6+

MATERIALS NEEDED

- Sturdy poles
- Paracord or rope

Did you know the earliest evidence of nails was found by archaeologists in Egyptian tombs? They were made from bronze and looked much like our metal nails do today. But what did people do before metal nails or even wooden pegs were invented to hold together wooden structures? The answer is that they used rope!

Rope isn't a very efficient tool unless you know how to use it. It is the skill to tie knots and fashion lashings that turns rope into something capable of doing amazing things. From building rafts strong enough for ocean travel to erecting tree houses in the jungle, rope (and the knowledge to use it), was once an indispensable tool used for countless construction projects. Knot tying is a life skill worth practicing. In fact, one of the bestselling books about knots lists over 3,900 different ones!

Even in a world dominated by metal nails, powerful ratcheting straps, and rubber bungee cords, it is important for every woodsman or woodswoman to have a basic understanding of ropework, especially when it comes to building structures like shelters. When using rope to securely lash together poles in any configuration you desire, one of the foundational skills you must learn is the square lashing.

In this project I'll teach you step-by-step how to tie the square lashing. The square lashing is used specifically to lash two poles together at a right angle (imagine a + symbol). With just this one lashing, you can erect an infinite number of structures in the wild or your backyard. You'll be limited only by your imagination, the amount of rope you have, or the number of sticks or poles available. In just an afternoon, a watchtower can be built from a pile of sticks and a spool of rope.

The size of the sticks will be a determining factor in the size and stability of the structure you can build. If you live on a farm with a forest nearby, getting these might not be a problem. But for most, long thick poles are hard to come by. However, don't let this stop you from learning! Even if you can't build a large tower, use the sticks that you have to build what you can. Miniature towers using pencils can be just as fun to build as larger towers in the backyard.

INSTRUCTIONS

Step 1: To start your square lashing, place one pole at a right angle across another. Now, tie a clove hitch around the bottom pole as shown. A clove hitch is very simple to tie. All you do is wrap the rope around the pole two and a half times. The first wrap goes all the way around. The second wrap goes all the way around as well, only it crosses over the first wrap to make an X shape with the rope. As the second wrap goes under the pole and comes up for the last half wrap, the tail goes underneath the middle of the X that is made by the first and second wrap. Then pull tight.

Step 2: Now for the wrapping. Wrapping is when you wrap the rope around the poles. Using the photo as a reference, wrap your rope in an over-under pattern around each leg of the cross. You will do this three times.

Step 3: Three sets of wraps are now in place. Tighten them up.

Step 4: Now for the frapping. Frapping is when you wrap the rope around rope to tighten the wraps that you just finished. Frapping is the key to a tight lashing. Instead of continuing the wrapping pattern, take the working end of the rope around the right cross leg and frap it around the middle of the two poles, wrapping only around the rope in the middle. You will do this three times.

Step 5: Three sets of fraps are now in place. Pull them as tight as you can.

Step 6: Finish with another clove hitch on the right-hand pole.

Square lashing at intersection of two poles on a tower.

Square lashing in action on a full-sized tower at Maumee Scout Reservation in Indiana.

PARENT'S GUIDE

Safety Notes

- If you're building a tower for climbing, I recommend using either 550 paracord, which has a tensile stretch of 550 pounds, or 1/4-inch diameter Manila rope. Manila rope of this size is commonly used in Scout pioneering projects for erecting towers and the like.

- Towers for climbing are only as strong as the poles used to build them. Climbing towers should be lashed using stout poles with 2 inches of diameter or larger. Dead and weak wood will make dangerous towers.

- A great way to start a climbing tower is to bury the bottom of the four corner posts in the ground a couple of feet. This not only sturdies the tower but holds them in place to lash the cross bars.

Tips to Improve Engagement

- For many people, full towers aren't practical. But many structures are possible with much smaller sticks and poles. Ladders, chairs, tables, and ottomans can all be built using just the square lashing. Use the sticks you have available to make some kind of structure.

- Schedule a Lashing Competition. In my own training experience, using mini competitions to teach knots and lashings is very effective. Challenge your children to see who can tie a square lashing correctly the fastest. Or judge the final lashing based on stability.

TEMPLATE

Bird-Watching Journal

BIRD NAME

DRAW A COLORED PICTURE OF THE BIRD

MALE OR FEMALE

FEATHER COLORS

DESCRIBE THE BIRD'S BEHAVIOR
(mean, shifty, nice, cautious, etc.)

TIME OF DAY OBSERVED

LOCATION

OTHER NOTES

ABOUT THE AUTHOR

CREEK STEWART is an expert survival instructor and the author of *Survival Hacks*, *The Disaster-Ready Home*, and the bestselling Build the Perfect Bug Out series of books. Creek has hosted three television programs on The Weather Channel: *Fat Guys in the Woods*, *SOS: How to Survive*, and *Could You Survive? with Creek Stewart*. Creek has been featured as a guest expert in numerous media outlets, including the *Today* show, *Fox & Friends*, *The Doctors*, *Men's Fitness*, *Backpacker*, and *Outdoor Life*. Creek is the owner and founder of Willow Haven Outdoor Survival Training School located in central Indiana, and APOCABOX, a bimonthly survival subscription box that ships to thousands of loyal subscribers every other month. He is the recipient of the prestigious Outstanding Eagle Scout Award bestowed by the Boy Scouts of America to Eagle Scouts who have demonstrated outstanding achievement at the local, state, or national level. Creek lives in central Indiana with his wife, Sarah, and two children, River and Lakelyn.

INDEX

A

Animal tracks, casting, 18–21
Animal tracks, identifying, 19–21
Arrowheads, abrading, 109–12
Art activities
    animal track casts, 18–21
    clay harvesting, 22–25
    clay whistle, 26–29
    gnome rocks, 30–33
    nature art, 13–37
    walnut dye T-shirt, 14–17
    wildflower crown, 34–37

B

Backpack essentials, 9–12
Bacon, cooking, 76–79
Baking techniques, 80–87
Basket making, 101–4
Bird feeders, 55–58
Birds, attracting, 55–58
Birds, identifying, 58, 139
Bonds, strengthening, 6–7, 92, 119
Braiding techniques, 35–36, 50
Bread, baking, 84–87
Bricks, making, 130–33
Bull-roarer, making, 43–46

C

Campfire safety, 75, 79, 114–16
Campfire, starting, 74–75, 113–16
Cans, metal, 72–75, 94–96
Carving tips, 43–46, 59–62, 85–86, 105–8
Cattail duck decoy, 47–50

Cell phones, 6, 10–11, 44
Charcoal, 94–96
Children
    bonding with, 6–7, 92, 119
    engaging, 6–9, 17, 21
    enjoying nature, 6–12
    less screen time for, 6
    memories for, 6–9, 35, 38, 63, 67, 117, 125
    parent-child relationship, 6–12
    respecting nature, 6–7, 92, 119
    sense of wonder for, 6–7, 33, 75, 116
Clay, harvesting, 22–25
Clay whistle, 26–29
Clothing, 9–10, 14–17
Conservation tips, 37, 42
Cooking sticks, 84–87
Cooking techniques, 72–87
Creativity
    art activities, 13–37
    encouraging, 6–8, 13, 108, 127, 132
    leaf rubbings, 39–42, 104
    soap carvings, 59–62
Crown, weaving, 34–37
Curiosity, 6–7, 31

D

Dandelion fritters, 65, 67
Dandelion tea, 64–67
Debris hut, 118–21
Distress signal, 29
Duck decoy, 47–50

E

Edible plants, 35–37, 63–71

Eggs, cooking, 76–79

Emergency supplies, 9–12, 62, 106

Engagement, improving, 6–9, 17, 21. *See also* Parent's Guide

Exploration, inspiring, 6–7, 13

F

Face carvings, 59–62

Family bonds, 6–7, 92, 119

Family relationships, 6–12

Ferro rods, 74, 113–16

Fire safety, 75, 79, 114–16

Fire, starting, 74–75, 113–16

Fire tinder, 75, 114–16

First aid kit, 10, 62. *See also* Survival kit

Fish trap, 97–100

Fishing bait, 88–91

Fishing reel, 105–8

Flashlights, 10

Flint strikers, 114

Food

    bacon, 76–79

    baking tips, 80–87

    cooking tips, 72–87

    dandelion fritters, 65

    dandelion tea, 64–67

    edible plants, 35–37, 63–71

    eggs, 76–79

    fish, 88–91, 97–100, 105–8

    foraging for, 63–67

    gardens, 68–71

    muffins, 80–83

    snacks, 9–10

    stick bread, 84–87

    stoves for, 15–16, 72–75

Foraging tips, 63–67

Fun and games

    bull-roarer, 43–46

    cattail duck decoy, 47–50

    leaf rubbings, 39–42

    pine cone bird feeder, 55–58

    soap carvings, 59–62

    tennis ball sling, 51–54

    types of, 38–62

G

Garden, planting, 68–71

Gear and tools

    arrowheads, 109–12

    emergency supplies, 9–12, 62, 106

    ferro rods, 74, 113–16

    fire starters, 74–75, 113–16

    fish trap, 97–100

    fishing hand reel, 105–8

    flint strikers, 114–15

    hammerstones, 110–12

    leaf basket, 101–4

    metal matches, 114–15

    pine pitch glue, 93–96

    shelters, 117–38

    stone tools, 109–12

    vagabond stove, 72–75

Glue, making, 93–96

Gnome rocks, painting, 30–33

H

Hammerstones, 110–12

Hand reel, making, 105–8

Hand reel template, 106–8

Hut, building, 118–21

I

Insects, identifying, 10, 91, 121

Inspiration, 6–7, 13

J

Journals

    benefits of, 39–40

    bird watching journal, 55–58, 139

leaf rubbing journal, 39–42, 104

nature journals, 39–42, 55–58, 104, 139

template page for, 139

K

Knife blades, 43–46, 60–62, 85–86, 106–12

Knots, tying, 36–37, 45–54, 128–29, 134–38

L

Lashing technique, 134–38

Leaf basket, 101–4

Leaf rubbings, 39–42, 104

Leaf rubbings journal, 39–42, 104

M

Matches, 114–15

Memories, creating, 6–9, 35, 38, 63, 67, 117, 125

Metal cans, 72–75, 94–96

Metal matches, 114–15

Metal strikers, 114–15

Milk carton garden, 68–71

Minnows, catching, 88–91

Mud and straw bricks, 130–33

Muffins, baking, 80–83

N

Nature

benefits of, 6–12

engaging with, 6–9, 17, 21

enjoying, 6–12

respect for, 6–7, 92, 119

versus screen time, 6

sense of wonder and, 6–7, 33, 75, 116

Nature art, 13–37. *See also* Art activities

Nature journals, 39–42, 55–58, 104, 139. *See also* Journals

Nets, making, 88–91

O

Online resources

animal track identification, 21

bird watching journal, 58

clay whistle, 29

edible plants, 35, 37, 67

ferro rods, 114

hand reel template, 107

leaf rubbings, 41

plant identification, 35, 37, 67

slate knife blade, 112

slings, 53–54

tarp shelters, 129

tick test, 10

tying knots, 129

walnut uses, 17

Outdoor activities. *See also specific activities*

benefits of, 6–12

food and foraging, 63–91

fun and games, 38–62

gear and tools, 92–116

nature art, 13–37

preparing for, 6–12

shelters, 117–38

P

Packing list, 9–12

Paint stick hand reel, 105–8

Paper bag cooking, 76–79

Parent-child bonds, 6–7, 92, 119

Parent-child relationship, 6–12

Parent's Guide, 7, 11, 17. *See also specific activities*

Phones, 6, 10–11, 44

Pine cone bird feeder, 55–58

Pine pitch glue, 93–96

Pine sap, 94–96

Plans, sharing, 10

Plants

edible plants, 35–37, 63–71

growing, 68–71

identifying, 15, 35, 37, 39–42, 50, 66–67, 121

milk carton garden, 68–71

poisonous plants, 35, 37, 42, 50, 121

Plastic bottles, reusing, 97–100

Pocketknife, 43–46, 60–62, 85–86. *See also* Knife blades
Preparations, making, 6–12

Q

Quinzee snow shelter, 122–25

R

Rescue signal, 29
Rocks, painting, 30–33

S

Safety glasses, 46, 111–12
Safety tips, 7, 10–11, 17, 46, 111–12. *See also* Parent's
  Guide
Sanitizers, 10, 69
Screen time, reducing, 6
Shelters
    debris hut, 118–21
    mud and straw bricks, 130–33
    Quinzee snow shelter, 122–25
    tarp shelter, 126–29
    tower, 134–38
    types of, 117–38
Shepherd's sling, 51–54
Sintering process, 123–24
Slate abrading process, 109–12
Sling, making, 51–54
Sling template, 52–53
Snacks, 9–10
Snow shelter, 122–25
Soap carvings, 59–62
Spiders, identifying, 91
Spiderweb nets, 88–91
Square lashing technique, 134–38
Stick bread, baking, 84–87
Stone tools, 109–12
Stove, making, 72–75
Stoves, outdoor, 15–16, 72–75
Strikers, flint, 114
Strikers, metal, 114–15
Supervision, 11, 17. *See also* Parent's Guide

Supply list, 9–12
Survival fishing reel, 105–8
Survival kit, 9–12, 62, 106
Survival shelters, 117–38. *See also* Shelters
Survival whistle, 28–29

T

Tarp shelter, 126–29
Tea, brewing, 64–67
Templates
    bird watching journal, 139
    hand reel template, 106–8
    journal template page, 139
    sling template, 52–53
Tennis ball sling, 51–54
Tie-dying technique, 17
Tin cans, 72–75, 94–96
Tinfoil, 75, 81–83
Tools, 92–116. *See also* Gear and tools
Tower, building, 134–38
Trees, identifying, 15, 39–42
T-shirt, walnut dye, 14–17
Tulip poplar leaf basket, 101–4
Twist bread, 84–87

V

Vagabond stove, 72–75

W

Water bottle fish trap, 97–100
Water supply, 9
Weather conditions, 9, 10
Weaving techniques, 34–37, 47–50, 89–91
Whistle, making, 26–29
Wilderness shelters, 117–38. *See also* Shelters
Wildflower crown, weaving, 34–37
Wonder, sense of, 6–7, 33, 75, 116